D1167698

OWLS

OWLS

A Wildlife Handbook

Kim Long

SCIENTIFIC ADVISOR
Bill Alther, zoologist

Johnson Books
BOULDER

294 2035

REMOVED
FROM
COLLECTION

WEST ISLIP PUBLIC LIBRARY
3 HIGBIE LANE
WEST ISLIP, NEW YORK 11795

Copyright © 1998 by Kim Long

All rights reserved. No part of this publication may be reproduced or transmitted in any form or by any means, electronic or mechanical, including photocopy, recording, or any information storage and retrieval system, without permission in writing from the publisher.

Published in the United States by Johnson Books, a division of Johnson Publishing Company, 1880 South 57th Court, Boulder, Colorado 80301.

9 8 7 6 5 4 3 2 1

Cover design: Margaret Donharl
Cover illustration: Kim Long

All illustrations by the author unless otherwise indicated.

Library of Congress Cataloging-in-Publication Data

Long, Kim.
  Owls: a wildlife handbook / Kim Long
      p. cm. — (Johnson nature series)
  Includes bibliographical references and index.
  ISBN 1-55566-200-5 (alk. paper)
      1. Owls. I. Title. II. Series: Long, Kim. Johnson nature series
QL696.S83L65 1998   98-2578
598.9'7—dc21   CIP

Printed in the United States by
Johnson Printing
1880 South 57th Court
Boulder, Colorado 80301

CONTENTS

ACKNOWLEDGMENTS

Dr. Randall Lockwood, Humane Society of the U.S.
Gregory McNamee
Michael McNierney
Bill Alther, Denver Museum of Natural History
Kathleen Cain
Greg Goodrich
Guy Hodge
The Bloomsbury Review
Denver Public Library
Norlin Library, University of Colorado
Auraria Library, Metropolitan State College
The Tattered Cover

INTRODUCTION

Owls are more than just another kind of bird to most people. Known throughout the world, they are at the same time strange and mysterious because even though they are present, they are rarely seen. Silent creatures of the night for the most part, cultures throughout history have linked them to unnatural forces and, often, death.

Yet despite their ominous spirit, they represent one of the more specialized and efficient group of hunters in the animal kingdom. With eyes and ears highly adapted to identify and locate prey, and feathers that generate no noise in flight, they have been largely successful in finding supportive habitats in almost every ecosystem on the planet, including some habitats altered by human civilization. Wherever populations of small rodents, birds, and other small creatures thrive, owls are likely to fill a niche at the top of the food chain.

In North America, however, the steady toll of grasslands, deserts, and forests lost to parking lots, shopping malls, and subdivisions, has pushed many owls out of their traditional homes and in some places, endangered their survival. And this loss comes at great expense to the natural balance of life, as owls have long provided a necessary limit to overpopulation by many of the animals they feed upon. As with many other newly-appreciated facets of the natural world, however, a brighter future may await these magnificent feathered predators as a wider audience develops an awareness that as elsewhere in nature, form, function, and beauty are often found in the same package.

THE TALE OF THE OWL

"Since the dawn of history, owls have been the pitiable victims of ignorance and superstition. Hated, despised and feared by many peoples, only their nocturnal habits have enabled them to survive in company with civilized man. In the minds of mankind they have been leagued with witches and malignant evil spirits, or even have been believed to personify the Evil One." — Edward Howe Forbush (1939)

Throughout the cultural history of the world, owls and the concept of death have often been linked. With few exceptions, people have been more inclined to associate these birds with the forces of evil than of good, and not until recent generations have owls achieved a more wholesome stature, becoming a symbol of wisdom and knowledge. The link between owls and death, however, is not hard to understand. A mysterious creature of the night, owls flew unseen while people slept and savagely attacked small animals and birds, many of whom symbolized spiritual harmony with nature and local gods. One of the few historical exceptions to this animosity and fear were the residents of early Athens, who from the beginning revered owls and associated them with Athena, one of their chief deities.

For most cultures, however, owls were ominous. In ancient Babylon, for example, the hoot of an owl at night came to represent the cries of a woman who died during childbirth, searching for her lost child. In Hungary, the owl was actually called the bird of death.

In ancient Egypt, owls were official symbols of death. The hieroglyphic for owl also symbolized night, cold, and a state of passivity. In addition, the written mark for owl could be used as a symbol for the sun after it had set, signifying in the Egyptian understanding of the cosmos the time when it was crossing through the darkness.

OWL PUNISHMENT

In Greek myths, Ascelpius was the son of Acheron, the river god in Hades, the underworld. One day, Ascelpius witnessed Persephone, the daughter of Demeter, as she was secretly eating pomegranate seeds. This was a serious mistake, as Persephone had been granted permission to leave the underworld, but only if she ate no food. Ascelpius tattled on Persephone to Pluto, the main god in Hades, who punished Persephone by only allowing her to leave Hades for part of every year. This punishment incensed Persephone's mother and in a fit of revenge, she changed Ascelpius into an owl. The same myth was part of the Roman tradition, with Ascalaphos the tattler, Ceres the pomegranate-eater, and Jove the god who meted out justice.

Lei-gong was a god of thunder in traditional Chinese mythology. The image created for this god was a body in the shape of a human with owl wings, claws, and beak. Owls in China were called "the birds who snatched away souls."

In Athens, owls were a plentiful part of the local wildlife and to Athenians, they represented a force of mystery, but one associated with good. Athene, the goddess of night, was symbolized by the owl and became associated with war, wisdom, and the liberal arts. In Buddhism, as well, the owl is an enemy of ignorance; it represented the isolation and darkness needed for deep meditation.

In ancient Rome, on the other hand, owls were apparently rarely seen. When someone did spot one of these birds during the day, it was considered an extremely unlucky omen. The appropriate antidote was to catch the owl and burn it, then scatter the ashes in the Tiber River. According to legend, before Caesar was

"An owl fighting with other birds." A woodcut created by Albrecht Durer about 1515 A.D.

murdered, owls were heard making their mournful cries. Agrippa and Augustus, among other legendary Romans, had misfortune befall them after encounters with owls.

A special group of priests in Rome were known as the augures, or augurs. Their role was a special one — to conduct ritual observations in order to determine if a specific event was approved by the gods. One of these rituals involved dividing the space visible from a hill into quadrants, and waiting to see what animals might appear. The same animal could mean different things, depending on where it appeared. The left, or east, represented light and was considered lucky. The right, or west, on the other hand, represented darkness and was unlucky. From various directions, the augurs watched for crows, eagles, vultures, and other birds, each type representing a different message. Owls were considered different from other birds in this ritual observation because they could deliver a portentous message not only through the pattern of their flight, but the sound of their hooting. And unfortunately for the owls, the only messages they were thought to deliver contained bad news.

In some other European cultures, owls were referred to as "night-ravens." Night-ravens are mentioned in the writings of Aristotle, some early Hebrew texts, throughout early English literature, and in works written by Spenser and Milton, among others. Whether called owl or night-raven, the image was not positive. Owls almost always represented evil, darkness, and death. In Celtic mythology, for example, Blodeuwedd, the flower-wife of Llew, was turned into an owl as punishment for conspiring to kill her husband.

In more than one culture, owls were also often portrayed as ene-mies of crows. In Hindu mythology, for example, owls waged war against the crows; one of the Hindu names for owl is kâkâris, or enemy of crow. The battle between owls and crows was also de-scribed by Aristotle, who blamed owls for using the cover of dark-ness to steal and eat eggs from the nests of crows. Myths about this rivalry lasted into modern times in parts of Europe.

Modern religions also have reference to these old beliefs. In some early Christian sects, the owl represented deception and was linked to Satan. In the old testament of the Bible, the only mention of owls is in the book of Isaiah. "The satyr shall cry to his fellow; the screech owl also shall rest there, and find for herself a place of rest" (Isaiah 34:14).

In Jewish folklore, Lilith was symbolized as an owl, a nasty spirit that flew around in the night and snatched children. Literally, her name in Hebrew means "Night Monster." In some Hebrew litera-ture, Lilith was depicted as the first wife of Adam or as Adam's mate after his marriage to Eve was ended with the eviction from Eden. In either case, Lilith bore several children, all of them demons. Lilith's evil nature has an even longer history, however. In the ancient kingdom of Sumeria, Lilith first appeared as the goddess of the underworld, depicted in carvings and statues as a woman with

OWL HERALDRY

Heraldry is a traditional system of designs and symbols used to denote family tradition in England and Europe. Birds and other animals are frequently used in heraldry and typically symbolize a desirable characteristic. Some family crests included owls, always shown facing forward. Traditionally, the owl was used to symbolize wisdom, intelligence, vigilance, and wit, but it was also once thought to symbolize laziness and cowardice in battle, possibly why few family crests before modern times included an image of this bird. English families with owls in their crests include Baldwin, Campbell, Hewlett, Milner, Moynihan, Russell, and Selby.

ARUNDEL

DAVIES

LEES

wings and talons. Lilith is also thought to be linked to Babylon, whose ancient culture existed after the Sumerians. In Babylon, she appeared as the female demon named Lilit. And Lilit herself was a form of the "Divine Owl Lady," a goddess known to the Sumerians as Inanna and to the Babylonians as Ishtar. Images of Inanna-Ishtar depict a woman surrounded by owls and with owl talons for feet.

In the Western Hemisphere, owls have also long been a part of cultural histories. In South America, the Mayans placed special emphasis on owls as a symbol of death. The traditional Mayan image of death included an underworld with nine levels. The lowest of these levels was Hunhau and it was ruled by Ah Puch, the God of Death. Ah Puch was symbolized by three animals: the dog, the moan bird, and the owl. Although linked to this underworld, Aztecs thought that owls were endowed with godly power.

The Aztec deity Techlotl was portrayed as an owl and Mictlantecutli, the ruler of the lowest layer of the underworld, had an owl, a bat, and a spider as symbols.

An owl god named Paupueo also existed in Hawaiian mythology. Originating on Kauai, Paupueo was a beneficial deity who organized all the owls on the island to help chase the Menehune — tiny,

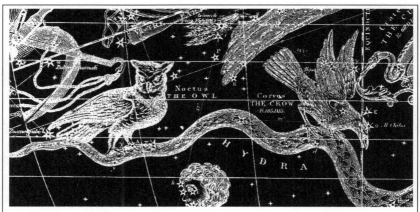

Although no longer an official constellation, Noctus, the Night Owl, was once part of the stellar map, at least according to European astronomers. Found near the tail of Hydra, to the left of the Owl are the scales of Libra and up and to the right is Virgo. Noctus, also known as Noctua, was first added to the constellation list in 1752 by Nicolas-Louis de Lacaille (1713–1762), a French astronomer. This illustration is from a star atlas published by Elijah Hinsdale Burritt in 1833.

leprechaun-like creatures — back into the caves and forests when they become too mischievous.

The Gran Chaco, a native culture in central South America, believes the voice of the owl brought a special message. It said, "Beware! I am bringing spirits to harm you." Far away in ancient Arabia, owls brought a similar message. A traditional Arab belief was that the spirits of people who had been murdered resided in owls. In their unique call the birds would speak of vengeance, "Give me to drink." And in Arabic, the name for owls is, in fact, derived from the words for "skull" and "echo."

The Kalmyks, one of the nomadic tribes of Mongolia, revered the owl because of local legend. According to their mythology, Genghis Khan, the founder of the Mongol empire, was saved by an owl when it perched on a small tree that was hiding him during an attack. The enemy, believing that no owl would perch close to where someone might be hiding, did not search the tree, thus saving the life of the Mongol leader. Owls were thereafter honored for their part in the leader's escape. The Tartars, also part of the Mongolian tradition, used feathers from male owls as amulets. To them, owls were an evil omen, usually meaning death, and the amulets were worn as a kind of "homeopathic" protection, using the power of one bird to keep other owls away.

In southeastern Australia, the Wotjobaluk tribe believed that owls were a major influence in the lives of women, tied to them by a spiritual force. The connection here, however, was more than that between a woman and all owls; each woman was "bound up" with the life of an individual owl. During her life, therefore, as each woman actively protected all owls from harm, she was helping to protect her own life and that of all other woman. The owl was in a literal sense a sister and was often called that. In the same tribe, men were bound up with the lives of bats.

NATIVE AMERICAN OWLS

"You should know that owls, after repaying their former debts, are reborn as wayward men in the realm of human beings." — *The Surangama Sutra* (8th Century A.D.)

Just as with cultures elsewhere in the world, owls were a symbol of mystery and death to Native Americans. Not just a bird, but one that flew at night, the owl often represented forces linked to darkness. For some tribes, this was considered a positive force, for others it was negative.

The Papago people believed that the owl caused sleepiness and associated the owl with the dead. The Southern Arapahoe believed that when dead, people went "upward" and some turned into owls. The Coast Salish and Nootkan tribes also placed special interpretation on the owl. In their cultures, too, the spirits of the dead become owls. Kiowas believed that only medicine men would turn into owls after they died. And after the owls died, the Kiowas believed they turned into crickets. Seminoles believed that only certain individuals turned into owls.

For Apache tribes, the owl was the symbol of a god known as "Big Owl." This deity, however, was evil and destructive. In their myths, other gods have confrontations with Big Owl but always win by outwitting him. For the Apache, Big Owl was dull and slow-witted, not the symbol of wisdom and intelligence.

In a myth from the Creek tribe, owls were portrayed as a devilish animal. According to the myth, one day a hunter stopped to camp near a thicket. At night, an owl came and hooted at the man. The owl scolded the man because he believed the man wanted to steal the owl's wife. The man and the owl argued, then the owl attacked the man, beat him, and scratched his face.

Among the Kutenai, the story of Coyote and Owl was a traditional tale. Once, a child kept crying. He was told to be quiet, or he

THE ORIGIN OF THE SCREECH OWL

According to a traditional myth of the Tlingit tribe, this is the story of how the screech owl was created. A woman lived with her husband and mother-in-law, whom she did not like. The people of the village saw that they did not get along and that the woman did not treat her mother-in-law with respect. One day the woman had a canoe-load of herring to unload and needing help, she shouted up to the village, "Bring me down my basket." But no one felt like helping her. She shouted louder and louder. Then the people heard her voice become strange as she repeated, over and over, "Hadé wudîkat, wudîkat, wudîkat ..." (This way with the basket, this way with the basket). Then they heard the sound of hooting. Soon, there was no more shouting, only the sound of hooting. Thus was born the screech owl. Today, when a young woman is seen to be selfish, the people tell her she may hurt her mother-in-law and as punishment, become an owl.

— adapted from *Tlingit Myths and Texts*
1909, Bureau of American Ethnology/Smithsonian Institute

would be taken away by Owl. But the child kept on crying and Owl did come. He put the child in a birch-bark basket and took him away. Then there were no more children and this caused Coyote to begin crying. He was told to be quiet or he too would be taken away by the owl. But Coyote kept on crying. As promised, the owl came, put him in a birch-bark basket, and took him away. Carrying Coyote, Owl arrived at his tent, where there were many children. But then Coyote smeared spruce gum on Owl's eyes, making him blind and threw him into the fire, burning him up. Then all the children returned to their parents.

One Eskimo folktale is about two owls hunting at night. The husband owl spotted two rabbits hunched close together and swooped down, snatching them both, one in each foot. But the two rabbits together were too big and strong for the owl to carry and they began to run over the ice, dragging the owl along. The owl's wife shouted to him to let one of the rabbits go. He couldn't, the husband owl responded, because it was about time for the moon to set, leaving them without enough light to hunt for more food. Meanwhile, the rabbits kept running, pulling the owl over the ice. They came to a large rock, where the two rabbits ran in different directions, one on each side of the rock. The owl, unwilling to let go, was torn in two.

A myth told by the Abnaki Indians tells of Gluskap and his twin brother Malsum, who did not get along with each other. Gluskap was the good brother; Malsum was evil. To protect himself, Gluskap lied to Malsum and told him that the only thing that could kill him was the stroke of an owl's feather. At night, Malsum shot Ko-ko-khas the owl with an arrow and touched Gluskap with it as he slept, but of course, Gluskap was not harmed. After more attempts on his life by Malsum, Gluskap killed his twin, turning him into an evil wolf. Then Gluskap was free to create the world.

A Winnebago creation myth assigns special significance to four deities, powerful sentinels who guarded the four primary directions. Manabozho was the wind and was found in the east; Menengwa was the butterfly and was found in the south; Animiki was the thunder and was found in the west; and Moho-koko-ko-ho was the owl and guarded the north. In Algonquin mythology, the owl was also credited with creating the north wind.

Special Kiowa medicine men were known as Owl Prophets, or "Maman-ti." The Kiowa had a special regard for the owl and its ability to know the future. Owl Prophets carried carefully preserved owl skins, usually from the screech owl, with which to interpret the

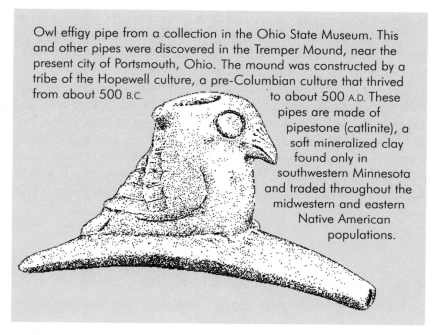

Owl effigy pipe from a collection in the Ohio State Museum. This and other pipes were discovered in the Tremper Mound, near the present city of Portsmouth, Ohio. The mound was constructed by a tribe of the Hopewell culture, a pre-Columbian culture that thrived from about 500 B.C. to about 500 A.D. These pipes are made of pipestone (catlinite), a soft mineralized clay found only in southwestern Minnesota and traded throughout the midwestern and eastern Native American populations.

owls' prophecies. The owl skin was sewn together so that it could be slipped over the hand of an Owl Prophet. A skillful medicine man would then "throw his voice" like a ventriloquist, making realistic owl sounds without moving his lips. This seer would then translate into Kiowa what the owl foretold for a particular individual.

Many other native cultures in North America also placed special meaning on the sighting or hearing of an owl. Among the Osage, for example, if an owl was heard hooting close to sunrise, the sound signified that the coming day would be clear and mild.

Among some Sioux tribes, the owl was considered sacred because it flew at night when people were asleep and dreaming, and the medicine man who obtained power from his dreams, wanted his dreams to be as clear as an owl's sight. Some Sioux medicine men wore owl feathers to concentrate their powers; they could not harm owls or they would lose their power. Cherokee warriors, to improve their night vision, washed their eyes with a solution made by soaking owl feathers in water and simmering over a fire.

Owl bones and feathers were sometimes part of medicine bundles and sacred packs used by tribal healers. The Chippewa and Fox tribes both used owl parts for their spiritual ceremonies. The Fox used an owl skin placed on a cornstalk that was fastened inside a lodge. Assembled when the corn was ripe, the skin, painted red, was used with a snapping turtle and a tortoise as a totem, to which tobacco was burned as an offering. If a person suddenly began "los-

THE GREAT GRAY OWL

Ho! little ones, he was heard to say, off in the distance,
He, the male great gray owl, lifted his voice and spoke,
He, whom we call grandfather.
At a time when the god of night was at his
      greatest strength,
He, whom we call grandfather,
With repeated calls, prolonged, lifted up his voice
      and spoke, saying:
I am one whose cries are ever listened to by Wa-kon'-da.
When the little ones make me a part of themselves,
Their cries, also, shall always be heard by Wa-kon'-da
When the little ones make me a part of themselves,
They shall be enabled throughout their life's journey to be
      heard by Wa-kon'-da.

      — Traditional Osage Indian ritual song

ing flesh," or wasting away, the Pima Indians believed the person might be afflicted with dreams about long-dead relatives. As a cure, the tribal healer used an owl's feathers to chase away the spirits of the departed. But owl powers were not confined just to healing. The Chippewa had a charm made with a dried owl skin. The owl charm could be "sent through the air" to cause an affliction on someone's lodge.

Members of the Pima tribe found special significance in owl feathers. They symbolized the next world and were given to people who were dying to help ease their transition from the present world. Among the Osage, Omaha, and Pawnee, owl feathers were also used as symbolic tokens on ritual smoking pipes. The traditional Osage pipe required three wing feathers, split full length. These feathered shafts were glued to the stem of the pipe to signify the power of the arrow. Owl feathers tied in a bunch might also be attached to the pipe, symbolizing the lungs of a deer. Pueblo cultures also commonly featured owls and owl feathers in religious rites. Some Kachina masks, for instance, required owl feathers as part of their ritual ornamentation.

The strength and hunting capabilities of this bird also made it special to warriors. In Cherokee tribes, warrior groups traditionally included three special scouts. One was Wolf, who scouted on the right, another was Fox, who scouted in the rear, and Owl scouted on the left.

OWL POWER: SUPERSTITIONS

"Whatever wise people may say of them, I at least myself have found the owl's cry always prophetic of mischief to me." — John Ruskin (*Praeterita,* 1889)

In many ancient cultures, owning or carrying a piece of an owl provided the carrier with special protections. Depending on the culture, appropriate parts included feet, feathers, eyes, hearts, bones, or even entire owl bodies. The power provided by these talismans ranged from avoidance of evil spirits to protection from health problems, including epilepsy and rabies. And protection was not the only power to be obtained; energy, wisdom, and bravery might also be imparted to the carrier.

Owl parts in a wide assortment were stocked and used by the professional healers of medieval Europe. Owl feet, burned with plumbago (graphite), were used as protection against serpents. The heart of the bird, carried by a warrior, strengthened him in battle; placed on the left breast of a sleeping woman, induced her to divulge secrets.

In some parts of India, owls were used as medicine for certain health conditions. Seizures in children could be treated with a broth made from owl eyes. Rheumatism pain was treated with a gel made from owl meat. Owl meat could also be eaten to arouse and extend sexual powers, a natural aphrodisiac. In northern India, folk tradition notes that if someone ate the eyes of an owl, they would, like the owl, be able to see in the dark.

In southern India, the cries of an owl were interpreted by number. One hoot was an omen of impending death; two meant success in anything that would be started soon after; three represented a woman being married into the family; four indicated a.disturbance; five denoted coming travel; six meant guests were on the way; seven was a sign of mental distress; eight foretold sudden death;

OWL SITES

Geographical locations in the United States named for the owl include more than 500 locations. "Owl" names on natural features of the landscape include variations such as "owlhead," "owl roost," "owl's nest," and "owl hoot."

- 2 arches
- 1 arroyo
- 1 bar
- 1 basin
- 3 bays
- 1 bayou
- 1 bend
- 87 canyons
- 4 capes
- 3 cliffs

- 194 creeks and streams
- 1 flat
- 8 gaps
- 2 islands
- 123 lakes
- 4 mountain ranges
- 15 springs
- 57 summits
- 5 swamps
- 87 valleys

and nine symbolized good fortune. In China, an owl's hooting represented the voice of demons.

Among early English folk cures, alcoholism was treated with owl eggs. The imbiber was prescribed raw eggs and a child given this treatment was thought to gain lifetime protection against drunkenness. Cooked until they turned into ashes, owls' eggs were also used as a potion to improve eyesight. According to an ancient Arabic treatise, however, owls' eggs had even more power. From each female owl supposedly came two eggs, one held the power to cause hair to fall out and one held the power to restore it.

An early Greek cure for gout: salted owl. And to cure epilepsy, a

Greek prescription was owl's egg soup made during a waning moon. In parts of South America, a folk cure for people recovering from illness was eating the flesh of the burrowing owl, thought to help generate an appetite.

Polish folklore links death with owls. Girls who die unmarried turn into doves; girls who are married when they die turn into owls. An owl cry heard in or near a home usually meant impending death, sickness, or other misfortune. In some regions of Europe, this was more specific. The owl hoots must come from a specific type of owl, a screech owl, for instance, and it must hoot a prescribed number of times. One example: If a screech owl was heard to hoot three times near where a sick person lay, they were sure to die soon. In order to cancel this outcome, the person hearing the owl was supposed to take off his or her shoes and turn them upside down.

Other "cures" for this sound of bad luck: throw salt over the shoulder or into the fire; tie a white string around a lock of hair; wear clothes backwards; turn pants pockets inside out; or lay a broom across the door. Another common European antidote for this predicament was to tie a knot in a handkerchief. A similar custom arose in India, where those who heard an owl call could counteract its supposedly evil effects by tying a knot in a woolen thread hanging from a beam inside a house. In India, however, the ritual was supposed to be performed while naked and a new knot added for each hoot.

Occasionally, the sound of an owl might also mean something positive. In some rural cultures, an owl hoot heard by a pregnant woman foretold the birth of a girl. Villagers in Wales and some other regions of ancient Britain, upon hearing a hoot, were certain it was the sign of a maiden losing her virginity.

In colonial New England and the southern states, owl hoots meant that bad weather was coming. If an owl "laughed," the weather would be fine. A variation on this weather forecasting method: bad weather was on the way if an owl was heard hooting on the east side of a mountain. In the Ozarks, traditional weather lore promised that an owl heard hooting in the daytime meant a storm was near. Rituals in more than one culture also relied on owls for protection from the weather. During the Roman empire and in more recent times in rural Germany, an owl — presumably dead — was nailed to a house door to divert hail and lightning. The very nature of the owl as an evil force provided people with an opportunity to use that force as a tool, as in "evil fights evil." This is one explanation used to describe how talismans and magic formulas gain significance in many cultures. In Japan, for example, owl carvings or figurines were used in homes as talismans to scare off disease and famine. According to Moroccan custom, an owl's eye worn on a string around the neck was an effective talisman to avert the "evil eye." And as immortalized by Shakespeare, witches in early western cultures not only consorted with owls, they used parts of owls to make various potions and brews.

OWL NAMES

"The names we humans give our wild neighbors are often misleading, inadequate, or unjust. Why call a silver-voiced songster a Screech Owl? A Screech Owl may chuckle, coo like a dove, or grunt like a tiny, arboreal pig; but his familiar song is a smoothly quavering whistle, so gently begun that it is well-nigh finished before we realize that our spine has tingled, our eyebrows lifted, our head turned, in response to the insistent cry."

— George Miksch Sutton (*Birds in the Wilderness,* 1936)

BARN OWL *Tyto alba.* Giovanni Scopoli, an Italian naturalist, officially described this bird in 1769 although it was widely known before this date. The species name "alba" also refers to the color white. Common names for the barn owl have included monkey-faced owl, ghost owl, church owl, death owl, hissing owl, hobgoblin or hobby owl, golden owl, night owl, rat owl, scritch owl, silver owl, straw owl, and white owl. In French Canada, this owl is known as *l'effraie* or *chat-huant.* In Mexico, it is *lechuza de campanario.*

BARRED OWL *Strix varia.* Benjamin Smith Barton (1766–1815), an amateur naturalist, published the first description of this owl in 1799. In Latin, "varia" is a form of the word "varius," meaning variegated or diverse. Common names for the barred owl include black-eyed owl, bottom owl, crazy owl, hoot owl, hooting owl, swamp owl, eight hooter, mouse owl, spotted owl, rain owl, and round-headed owl. In French-speaking Canada, the name is *chouette rayée* or *chat-huant.* In Mexico, it is called *búho barrado.*

BOREAL OWL *Aegolius funereus.* In 1758, Karl von Linné named this owl after Boreas, the Greek god of the north wind. Linné (1707–1778), a Swedish naturalist, is now commonly referred to as Linnaeus and was the father of the modern scientific classification

THE BIRD THAT HOOTS

The word owl originated in early European languages. In old Norse, for example, an owl was known as *ugla*; in old German, it was *uwila*. Both of these words might have been created as sounds that described the unique call of the owl. In Old English — the original form of the English language as it was used from about 600 A.D. to about 1000 A.D. — owl was *ule*, a world similar to the original Dutch word. In Middle English — in use from the end of the Old English period to roughly the 1400s — this became *owle*, later shortened to the form we use today. Along the way, various early written records also included variations on this spelling, including *uwile, oule, owell, hoole,* and *howyell*. Other ancient cultures also created words for owl that seem to describe the owl's hooting voice. In India, for example, owls were once known as *oo-loo* and in Hebrew, *o-ah*.

system. Many plants and animals — including the most common birds — were first "tagged" by Linnaeus although many of his original classifications have since been modernized. "Funereus" is from the Latin word that means funeral. Earlier names for this owl included Tengmalm's owl and Richardson's owl. Common names include American sparrow owl, little owl, and partridge-haw.

BURROWING OWL *Athene cuniculbria*. Giovanni Iganzio Molina (1740–1829) published the first report of the burrowing owl. Molina was a Jesuit priest from Italy stationed in Chile, where in 1782 he wrote a book on the natural history of the country, including a description of this bird. An appropriate description of its home

THE LANGUAGE OF OWLS

AFRIKAANS *uil*
AMHARIC *guggut*
ARABIC *búm, hàma sadā, hufj*
AZERBAIJANI *bayquş*
AZTEC *tecólotl*
BASQUE *gauhontza*
CZECHOSLOVAKIAN *sova*
CHINESE *māotóuyīng*
DANISH *slørugle*
DUTCH *uil*
ESPERANTO *strigo*
FRENCH *hibou, chouette*
GAELIC *ulchabhan*
GERMAN *eule, uhu*
GREEK *glaux, skops, buas, strix*
HAUSA *mujiya*
HAITIAN CREOLE *koukou*
HAWAIIAN *pueo*
HEBREW *yanshoof*
HINDI *ullū, ghughu*
HUNGARIAN *bagoly*
ITALIAN *gufo, strige*
JAPANESE *fukurou*
KAZAKH *üki*
KOREAN *ol-bbae-mi*
KIKUYU *ndundu*
KYRGYZ *ükü*

LAOTIAN *no:k kow:*
LATIN *ululu, strix, bubo, noctua*
MALAY *burong hantu*
MAORI *koukou, ruru*
MONGOLIAN *uuli*
NORWEGIAN *ugle*
PHILIPINO *kuwágo*
POLISH *sowa*
PORTUGUESE *coruja*
RUSSIAN *óïxá, sova*
SANSCRIT *uluka, kâkâris*
SERBO-CROATIAN *sova*
SOMALI *guumeys*
SOTHO *sephooko* (barn owl)
SPANISH *búho, lechuza*
SWAHILI *bundi*
SWEDISH *uggla*
TAGALOG *kuwago*
TARTAR *yabalak*
TURKISH *baykuş, puhu*
UIGHUR *müshük, yapilaq*
UZBEK *boyo'g'li*
YIDDISH *sove*
YORUBA *òwìwí*
ZULU *isikhova*

AMERICAN INDIAN LANGUAGES

APACHE *niishjaa'*

ARAWAK *hu-tu-tu*

ATAKAPA *wawact*

BILOXI *aphó*

BLACKFOOT *sipisttoo*

CHEROKEE *u gu gu, tskili*
(great horned owl)

CHOCTAW *opa*

COMANCHE *mupitz*

ESKIMO *anipa* (snowy owl)

DELAWARE *gōkhoos*

FOX *wītegowä*

HOPI *mongwu*

KIOWA *sop'oudl, beidl-kiHt`-gyH*
(screech owl)

KUTENAI *kúpe$_i$*

MAYA *tunkuruchu*

NAVAJO *né'éshjaa'*

OJIBWAY *gookooko´oo*

ONONDAGA *gachnichzohō*

OSAGE *pá nu hu*

PAPAGO *chukuD*

SENECA *ohohwa*

SHOSHONE *moobeech*

SIOUX *hiṇhaṇ´, hin-yan-ka-ga*

TUNICA *ú wa* (great horned owl)

ZUNI *mu-hu-que*

SIGN LANGUAGE

Among some North American tribes, the word for owl could be "spoken" with the hands in a universal sign language understood across many cultures. To make this sign, a person would first form the sign for bird, with fingers spread on each side of the body and flapped like a bird's wings. Then, thumbs and index fingers on both hands would be used to form circles and held over the eyes.

below ground, the Latin word "cunicularius," meaning mine or miner, was altered to fit this owl. Early European settlers in Florida sometimes referred to this bird as the Johnny owl or the ground owl. Other common names were badger-hole owl, gopher owl, billy owl, long-legged owl, prairie dog owl, prairie owl, and howdy owl. In French-speaking Canada, the name is *coucouterre* or *chouette à terrier*. In Mexico, it's *lechucillo, lechucita de las viscacheras,* or *búho llanero.*

"Kennicott's Owl," a wood engraving from *A History of North American Birds,* by Baird, Brewer, and Ridgway, published by Little, Brown, & Company in 1874.

ORDER AND FAMILY NAMES

STRIGIFORMES   All owls are classified as members of this order. The name is formed from "Strig-," the plural form of the Latin word "strix," meaning owl and "-formes," meaning forms.

STRIGOIDES   The family for all owls except barn owls, it is a combination of root words from both Latin and Greek. "Strix" is a Latin word for owl (also the same in Greek) and "oides" is a Greek word meaning "resembling."

TYTONIDAE   All barn owls are members of this family. The name is derived from the Greek word "tuto," which means owl.

GENUS NAMES

AEGOLIUS   A Latin word for bird of prey. It is also similar to the Greek word "aigolios," meaning a bird that is an evil omen.

ATHENE   One of the ancient Greek deities, originally known as the goddess of night. She was symbolized by the image of an owl. Over time, her role evolved into the goddess of war, wisdom, and the liberal arts.

GLAUCIDIUM   The diminutive form of the Greek word "glaux," or "little owl."

MICRATHENE   Formed from the Greek word "mikros," meaning "small."

NYCTEA   From the Greek word "nuktia," meaning "of the night."

OTUS   A variation of the original Greek word "otos," meaning owl.

TYTO   A variation of the Greek word "tuto," or owl.

EASTERN SCREECH OWL *Otus asio*. This screech owl is another bird that was first described by Linnaeus. He classified it in 1758. "Asio" is a Latin word that was used in the writings of Pliny the Elder, a Roman naturalist (circa 23 A.D.–79 A.D.) who wrote thirty-seven books about the natural world. Although the origin of the word is unknown, it came to mean "owl" in Latin. This owl has also been called the common screech owl, whickering owl, little gray owl, mottled owl, the red owl, the mouse owl, the cat owl, the shivering owl, and the little horned owl. In Florida, local names also included the squinch owl and the death owl. In French Canada, it is called *petit-duc d'amérique*, *chat haut*, or *chouette*. In Mexico, the name is *tecolote oriental*.

ELF OWL *Micrathene whitneyi*. The first published report of the elf owl came in 1861 from James Graham Cooper (1830–1902), a doctor and naturalist who participated in several geographic expeditions in the western states. Cooper was the son of William Cooper, a friend of John James Audubon, and is credited with writing the first book on the birds of California, published in 1870. "Whitneyi" is a Latinized word formed from the last name of Josiah Dwight Whitney (1819–1896), a prominent American geologist and the founder of the Harvard School of Mining in 1868. The elf owl was first known as Whitney's owl. In Mexico, it is called *enano*.

FERRUGINOUS PYGMY OWL *Glaucidium brasilianum*. The first account of this bird was published in 1788 and credited to Johann Georg Gmelin (1709–1755), a Russian naturalist and explorer. "Brasilianum" is a Latinized form of the Portuguese word "brasil," now referring to the South American country but originally it described a type of tree or wood that came from that part of the continent. For many years, this bird and the elf owl were officially known as Whitney's owls. In Mexico, the name is *tecolotito común*.

FLAMMULATED OWL *Otus flammeolus*. Johann Jakob Kaup (1803–1902) published the first information about this bird in

OWL WORDS

The word owl has been applied to many things, from other animals to pottery, including ...

owl-pigeon, sea owl, owl ray, owl barn, owl light, owl time, owl eye, owl hole, owl shooter, owl sight, owl's head, owl wing, owl headed, owl blasted, owl bus, owl catchers, owl jug, owl train, owl trolley, owl butterfly, owl-faced bat, owl-faced monkey, owl fly, owl gazelle, owl gnat, owl midge, owl moth, owl parrot, owl swallow, owl's crown, owl glass, owl head, owl clover, and owl moth.

1853. Kaup was a German scientist and the director of a zoological collection in Darmstadt, Germany. Derived from the Latin word for flame, or flame-shaped, "flammeolus" refers to the unique coloration of this bird. This owl is sometimes called the dwarf owl and was once called the flammulated screech owl. The French Canadian name is *petit duc nain* and in Mexico it's called *tecolotito* or *tecolote flameado*.

GREAT GRAY OWL *Strix nebulosa*. In 1772, Johann Reinhold Forster (1729–1798) published the first description of the great gray owl. Forster and his son Georg, both noted naturalists, sailed with Captain Cook on his second voyage around the world. "Nebulosus" is Latin for misty or foggy. The great gray has also been known as the gray ghost, speckled owl, spectral owl, lapland owl, the spruce owl, and the cinerous owl. In the French Canadian territory, the owl is called *chouette-cendrée*.

GREAT HORNED OWL *Bubo virginianus*. As this owl was first seen in the Virginia colonies, its species name was created as a Latinized

A woodcut illustration of a long-eared owl by Thomas Bewick, from A *History of British Birds*, published by Longman and Company in 1826.

form of the name of this territory, originally named for Queen Elizabeth I of England, the "Virgin Queen" (1533–1603). Johann Gmelin is credited with the first published description, in 1788. Common names for this owl included big cat owl, big hoot owl, chicken owl, horned owl, king owl, eagle owl, white owl, and winged tiger. French Canadians call it *le grand duc*; Mexicans refer to it as *búho real* or *búho cornudo*.

LONG-EARED OWL *Asio otus*. Linnaeus first described this owl in 1758, one of the earliest owls to be classified under his new system.

Common names include lesser horned owl, cedar owl, coulee owl, pussy owl, cat owl, and brush owl. In French Canada, it is called *hibou à oreilles*. In Mexico, it is known as *búho-cornudo caricafé*.

NORTHERN HAWK OWL *Surnia ulula*. Linnaeus described the hawk owl in 1758 and A.M.C. Duméril (1774–1860), a French zoologist, is given credit for coining its scientific name in 1806. The original meaning is not known, but "ulula" is one of the original Latin words for screech owl, cited by Pliny and others in ancient Roman texts. Common names include Canadian owl, day owl, hawk owl, falcon owl, stub owl, and tooting owl. In French Canada, the name is *chouette épervière*.

NORTHERN PYGMY OWL *Glaucidium gnoma*. Johann Wagler (1800–1832) described the northern pygmy owl in 1832. A German naturalist, Wagler was in charge of organizing the collections at the University of Munich. The species name "gnoma" is formed from the Latin word "gnomus," meaning gnome or dwarf, and the owl has been called the gnome owl in early years. The French-Canadian name is *chouette pygmée*. In Mexico, it is called *tecolotito serrano*.

Woodcut of short-eared owl from *American Ornithology* by Alexander Wilson. Published by Whittaker, Treacher & Arnot (London) in 1832.

NORTHERN SAW-WHET OWL *Aegolius acadius*. Johann Gmelin received credit for describing this owl in 1788. European explorers first spotted this owl in the North American colony of Acadia, now known as Nova Scotia. The Latinized word "acadius" refers to this territory. The saw-whet owl got its common name because of its unique vocal calls, reminding early observers of the sound of a file being used to sharpen a saw. Other names included Acadian owl, blind owl, Kirkland's owl, the saw-filer, the sawyer, sparrow owl, the white-fronted owl, and sometimes, contrarily, the whet-saw owl. A common name in the French Canadian provinces is *petite nyctale* or *chouette des granges*. In Mexico, it is called *tecolote-abetero norteño*.

SHORT-EARED OWL *Asio flammeus*. Erich Ludvigsen Pontoppidan (1698–1764), a Danish bishop and amateur naturalist, published the first description of this owl in 1763. In Latin, the word "flammeus" means fiery, flaming, or the color of fire. Local names for the short-eared owl include the evening owl, marsh owl, bog or swamp owl, grass owl, meadow owl, mouse-hawk, and flat-faced owl. In French Canada, the name is *hibou à oreilles courtes*. In Mexico, the name is *lechuza de sabana, mucaro real*, or *búho orejicorto*. This owl is also found in Hawaii, where it is known as *pueo*.

SNOWY OWL *Nyctea scandiaca*. The snowy owl was first classified by Linnaeus in 1758. Originally observed in the northern parts of Europe, the species name "scandiaca" is a Latinized word referring to Scandinavia. Common names include arctic owl, great white owl, ghost owl, and ermine owl. In French Canada, it is called *hibou blanc* or *harfang des neiges*.

SPOTTED OWL *Strix occidentalis*. John Xántus de Vesey (1825–1894), an Hungarian immigrant to the United States, reported the spotted owl in 1860. The Latin word "occidentalis" refers to something that is from the west; the Latin "occidens" means west or evening. Local and common names include canyon owl, brown-eyed owl, wood owl, and hooting owl. Earlier, the bird was sometimes known as the

Xántus owl or the Arizona spotted owl. In French Canada, it is *chathuant tacheté*. In Mexico, it is known as *búho manchado*.

WESTERN SCREECH OWL *Otus kennicotti*. The western screech owl was first described in 1867. The species name "kennicotti," was created to honor Robert Kennicott, an American explorer and naturalist (1835–1866) and originally, the official name for this bird was Kennicott's owl. Common names include little horned owl, dusk owl, ghost owl, mouse owl, and cat owl. In Mexico, it's called *tecolotito* or *tecolote occidental*.

WHISKERED SCREECH OWL *Otus trichopsis*. The scientific name for the whiskered screech owl was coined by Johann Wagler (1800–1832) in 1832, while he was employed organizing zoological collections at the University of Munich in Germany. "Trichopsis" is a combination of two Greek words, "thrix" meaning hair and "opsis" meaning face. Thus, the term refers to this owl's hairy or whiskered face. Another common name for this bird is spotted screech owl. The Mexican name is *tecolotito, manchado*, or *tecolote bigotudo*.

OWL SPECIES

SIZE COMPARISON

GREAT GRAY OWL

SNOWY OWL

GREAT HORNED OWL

FLAMMULATED OWL

WHISKERED SCREECH OWL

FERRUGINOUS PYGMY OWL

NORTHERN SAW-WHET OWL

BARN OWL

BARRED OWL

ELF OWL

BURROWING OWL

BOREAL OWL

LONG-EARED OWL

NORTHERN PYGMY OWL

NORTHERN HAWK OWL

SHORT-EARED OWL

SPOTTED OWL

WESTERN SCREECH OWL

EASTERN SCREECH OWL

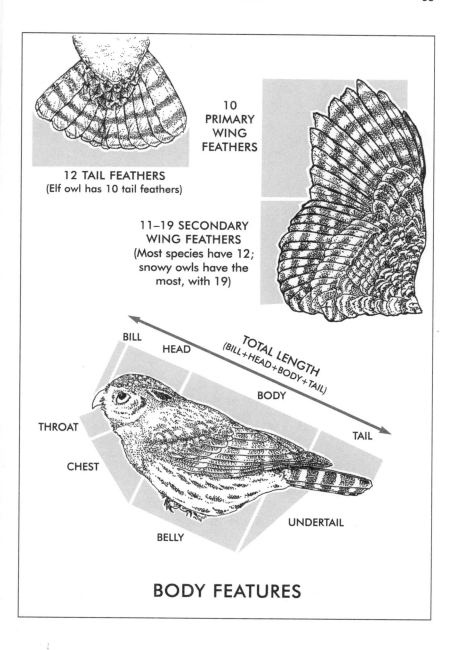

10
**PRIMARY
WING
FEATHERS**

12 TAIL FEATHERS
(Elf owl has 10 tail feathers)

**11–19 SECONDARY
WING FEATHERS**
(Most species have 12;
snowy owls have the
most, with 19)

BILL
HEAD
TOTAL LENGTH
(BILL+HEAD+BODY+TAIL)

BODY

THROAT

TAIL

CHEST

UNDERTAIL

BELLY

BODY FEATURES

BARN OWL

RANGE

Approximate normal range
of species.

● States where species is
occasionally sighted.

VITAL STATISTICS

NAME	**Barn owl** *Tyto alba* monkey-faced owl, hissing owl SPANISH lechuza de campanario FRENCH l'effraie
DESCRIPTION	Medium size; boxy shape with distinctive heart-shaped face. Bill pale in color; eyes dark with no yellow pigment. Body reddish brown on back, white to light brown on chest and belly, with brown spots; chest and belly white with darker markings; face white with dark border. Females slightly larger and darker in color than males.
COMPARISON	Distinctive heart-shaped face; usually lighter in color than other owls its size.

TOTAL LENGTH	14–21" 35.6–53.3 cm	WING LENGTH	12–14" 30.5–35.6 cm
WEIGHT	11–21 oz 299–580 gms	**TAIL LENGTH**	5–6" 12.7–15.2 cm

RANGE	Throughout U.S. and Mexico, Atlantic coast to Pacific coast, Mexico and Gulf of Mexico north to Canada except for upper plains states.
HABITAT	Common around human habitats, including farms, warehouses, stadiums, and other open structures.
HABITS	Nocturnal. 3–11 eggs (5 is average); incubated by female for 21–32 days, depending on size of brood; may raise 2 broods in one year; nests year-round. First flight: 56–62 days.
VOCAL CALL	Raspy hissing. Single shrill note.

BARRED OWL

RANGE

Approximate normal range
of species.

VITAL STATISTICS

NAME	**Barred owl** *Strix varia* hoot owl, wood owl FRENCH-CANADIAN chat-huant SPANISH búho barrado
DESCRIPTION	Large size; body shape broad and boxy. Bill pale in color; eyes are dark with no yellow pigment. No ear tufts. Body brown with dark highlights; chest and belly lighter in color with dark barring. Females larger than males.
COMPARISON	Similar in size and appearance to spotted owl, except without white spots behind head.

TOTAL LENGTH	16–24" 40.6–61 cm	**WING LENGTH**	12–14" 30.5–35.6 cm
WEIGHT	1–2 1/3 lbs 468–1051 gms	**TAIL LENGTH**	8–10" 20.3–25.4 cm

RANGE	Across central Canada and throughout eastern U.S. from Canada south to Gulf of Mexico, west through western plains. Also in northwest states.
HABITAT	Dense woods, swamps, conifers, hardwood and conifer-hardwood forests.
HABITS	Mostly nocturnal; may be heard during daytime. Prefers to stay in same nest area from year to year. 2–3 eggs; incubation by both parents for 28–33 days; 1 or 2 broods per year. First flight: about 40 days.
VOCAL CALL	Loud rhythmic song "hoo, HOO, hoo, hoo" sometimes with added "hooo-aaaah" at end.

BOREAL OWL

RANGE

Approximate normal range of species.

States where species is occasionally sighted.

VITAL STATISTICS

NAME	**Boreal owl** *Aegolius funereus* Tengmalm's owl, Richardson's owl, funereal owl
DESCRIPTION	Medium size. Bill pale in color; eyes with yellow pigment. Small, rounded ear tufts. Body dark brown; white chest and belly with brown barring; face white or lighter in color with dark to black border. Females slightly larger than males.
COMPARISON	Similar in color and pattern to saw-whet owl, except several inches larger, has pale-colored bill, and dark border around face.

TOTAL LENGTH	8–12" 20.3–30.5 cm	**WING LENGTH**	6¼–7" 16–17.8 cm
WEIGHT	3–6 oz 116–197 gms	**TAIL LENGTH**	3¾–4" 9.5–10.2 cm

RANGE	Throughout Canada and Alaska, south to Great Lakes and northern Rocky Mountains.
HABITAT	Conifer forests, bogs, thickets, mixed hardwood-conifer forests.
HABITS	Nocturnal. 3–6 eggs; incubation by females for 25–32 days. First flight: 28–36 days.
VOCAL CALL	Series of rapidly repeated short notes, "hoo, hoo, hoo, hoo ..."

BURROWING OWL

RANGE

Approximate normal range of species.

States where species is occasionally sighted.

VITAL STATISTICS

NAME	Burrowing owl *Athene cunicularia* gopher owl FRENCH CANADIAN chouette à terrier SPANISH búho llanero
DESCRIPTION	Small to medium size. Bill pale in color; eyes with yellow pigment. No ear tufts. Body brown in color with distinctive spots; chest and belly white to pale with brown barring. Legs are noticeably longer than other owls. Females and males about the same size.
COMPARISON	Characteristic long legs and activity on ground makes this owl distinct from other species.

TOTAL LENGTH	8½–11" 21.6–27.9 cm	**WING LENGTH**	6½–7" 16.5–17.8 cm
WEIGHT	4½–8 oz 120–228 gms	**TAIL LENGTH**	3–3½" 7.6–8.9 cm

RANGE	Year-round resident in southern areas of southwestern states from Pacific coast to Gulf of Mexico. Breeding range includes Sierras east through Rocky Mountains and western plains from southern Canada south to Mexico.
HABITAT	Open, untreed expanses, including mesas, prairies, and plains. May visit parks and golf courses.
HABITS	Nocturnal. Flies low to ground and uses hovering flight when stalking prey. Perches at entrance to burrow or nearby on low rises in daylight hours. 6–11 eggs; incubated by females for 21–30 days; 1 brood per year. First flight: 40–45 days.
VOCAL CALL	Chatter notes, "chack, chack, chack ..." and low, quiet "coo-coooo."

Red Phase

Gray Phase

EASTERN SCREECH OWL

RANGE

Approximate normal range of species.

States where species is occasionally sighted.

VITAL STATISTICS

NAME	**Eastern screech owl** *Otus asio* mouse owl, cat owl FRENCH CANADIAN petit duc SPANISH tecolote oriental
DESCRIPTION	Small owl. Bill pale gray in color. Ear tufts prominent when raised. Chest and belly barred, heavy barring on upper chest. Two color phases: red phase has distinctive reddish coloring over most of body; gray phase features gray color. Females larger than males.
COMPARISON	Similar to western screech owl, except bill is not black. Ranges overlap only in some areas of western plains, south to Texas.

TOTAL LENGTH	7–10" 17.8–25.4 cm	WING LENGTH	5½–6½" 13.9–16.5 cm
WEIGHT	4–8 oz 140–235 gms	**TAIL LENGTH**	2½–3" 6.4–7.6 cm

RANGE	Eastern U.S. and extreme southern Canada, from Atlantic coast west through plains, south to Gulf of Mexico.
HABITAT	Forests, swamps, foothills, valleys, deserts, also common in urban and suburban settings.
HABITS	Nocturnal. 3–5 eggs; incubated by female for 21–30 days; male feeds female during incubation. First flight: 30–32 days. Males and females mate for life, but will replace mates if one dies.
VOCAL CALL	Series of whistles in descending pitch. Single elongated trill.

ELF OWL

RANGE

Approximate normal range of species.

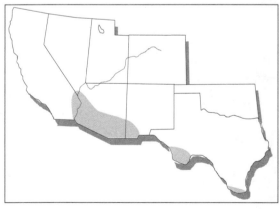

VITAL STATISTICS

NAME	**Elf owl** *Micrathene whitneyi* Whitney's owl **SPANISH** enano, tecolotito enano
DESCRIPTION	Smallest owl in North America. Bill pale in color; eyes with yellow pigment. Body short and boxy; color brown to gray-brown. No ear tufts. Tail short. Females and males are about the same size.
COMPARISON	Similar in size and appearance to ferruginous pygmy owl, except for shorter tail and lack of ear tufts.

TOTAL LENGTH	5–6" 12.7–15.2 cm	**WING LENGTH**	4–5" 10.2–12.7 cm
WEIGHT	1–1¾ oz 36–48 gms	**TAIL LENGTH**	1¾–2" 4.5–5.1 cm

RANGE	No permanent range north of Mexico. Breeding range extends throughout southern Arizona, southeastern California, southwestern New Mexico and extreme southwestern Texas.
HABITAT	Desert, lowlands and foothills, canyons, oak and sycamore stands.
HABITS	Nocturnal. Nests in saguaro cacti and trees. 2–5 eggs; incubated by female for 21–24 days. First flight: about 28 days.
VOCAL CALL	High-pitched "chirp, chirp" or chatter notes.

FERRUGINOUS
PYGMY OWL

RANGE

Approximate
normal range
of species.

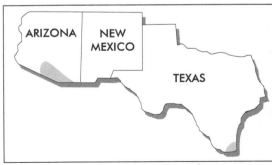

VITAL STATISTICS

NAME	**Ferruginous pygmy owl** *Glaucidium brasilianum* cactus pygmy owl **SPANISH** tecolotito común
DESCRIPTION	Small size. Body boxy in shape. Bill pale in color; eyes have yellow pigment. No ear tufts. Body brown to grayish-brown; chest and belly white with brown or reddish-brown streaks; distinctive black marks on back of head. Long tail. Females larger than males.
COMPARISON	Similar in size and coloring to northern pygmy owl but usually found in habitats at lower elevations.

TOTAL LENGTH	6–7" 15.2–17.8 cm	**WING LENGTH**	3½–4" 8.9–10.2 cm
WEIGHT	2–3 oz 46–87 gms	**TAIL LENGTH**	2–2¾" 5.1–7.0 cm

RANGE	Permanent range throughout central Mexico and along both coasts, north to extreme south central Arizona and extreme southern Texas near border.
HABITAT	Deserts, open woodlands, wooded streambanks.
HABITS	Diurnal, most active in early and late daylight hours. Flies with quicker wingstrokes than other owls and flight sounds are audible. 3–4 eggs; incubation is about 30 days. First flight: about 28 days.
VOCAL CALL	Rapid series of notes "took, took, took."

FLAMMULATED OWL

RANGE

Approximate normal range of species.

States where species is occasionally sighted.

VITAL STATISTICS

NAME	**Flammulated owl** *Otus flammeolus* **FRENCH-CANADIAN** petit duc nain **SPANISH** tecolote flameado
DESCRIPTION	Small size. Short, boxy shape. Small ear tufts. Bill gray in color; eyes dark, without yellow pigment. Body brown, dark gray, and reddish brown; chest and belly brown and gray with dark markings. Females larger than males.
COMPARISON	Only small owl in North America with dark eyes that lack yellow iris.

TOTAL LENGTH	6–7" 15.2–17.8 cm	**WING LENGTH**	5–5½" 12.7–13.9 cm
WEIGHT	1½–2½ oz 54–57 gms	**TAIL LENGTH**	2¼–2½" 5.7–6.4 cm

RANGE	No permanent range in North America. Breeding range throughout western states, north from Arizona and New Mexico into southern British Columbia.
HABITAT	Forests up to 10,000 feet, oak, ponderosa pine, other conifers, aspen, and mixed hardwood-conifer.
HABITS	Nocturnal. May form nesting colonies. 3–4 eggs; incubated by female for about 21–26 days; male feeds female during incubation. First flight: 22–25 days.
VOCAL CALL	Extended series of single hoots, also double hoot.

GREAT GRAY OWL

RANGE

Approximate normal range of species.

● States where species is occasionally sighted.

VITAL STATISTICS

NAME	**Great gray owl** *Strix nebulosa* spruce owl FRENCH-CANADIAN chouette-cendrée
DESCRIPTION	Largest owl in North America. Large head. No ear tufts. Bill pale in color; eyes with yellow pigment. Body brown with darker markings; chest and belly lighter brown to grayish-brown with darker markings; distinctive series of dark concentric rings around eyes. Females darker and larger than males.
COMPARISON	Similar to great horned owl in size but has distinctive rings around eyes and no ear tufts.

TOTAL LENGTH	24–33" 61–84 cm	**WING LENGTH**	16–18" 40.6–45.7 cm
WEIGHT	1¾–3½ oz 790–1454 gms	**TAIL LENGTH**	12–13½" 30.5–34.3 cm

RANGE	Alaska and western Canada east to Great Lakes. Northwestern U.S. and upper Great Lakes states.
HABITAT	Forests, meadows, and bogs. Prefers conifers.
HABITS	Diurnal. 2–5 eggs; incubated by female for about 28 days; male feeds female during incubation and brooding; 1 brood per year. First flight: about 55 days.
VOCAL CALL	Series of low, strong notes "hooo, hooo, hooo ..."

**GREAT HORNED
OWL**

RANGE

Approximate normal range
of species.

VITAL STATISTICS

NAME	**Great horned owl** *Bubo virginianus* FRENCH-CANADIAN le grand duc SPANISH búho real
DESCRIPTION	Large size. Large ear tufts. Bill dark in color; eyes with yellow pigment. Boxy shape. Body brown and grayish-brown with dark markings; throat white; chest and belly brown with regular darker markings; face reddish-brown with dark border. Pale color phase found in central Canada. Females larger than males.
COMPARISON	Similar in coloring to long-eared owl, but larger and boxier in shape.

TOTAL LENGTH	18–25" 45.7–63.5 cm	**WING LENGTH**	12–15½" 30.5–39.4 cm
WEIGHT	3–5 lbs 900–1800 gms	**TAIL LENGTH**	6¾–10" 17.2–25.4 cm

RANGE	Throughout Canada, Alaska, and all the lower 48 states.
HABITAT	Forests, desert, swamps, meadows, plains.
HABITS	Mostly nocturnal. 1–4 eggs; incubated mostly by female for 28–35 days. 1 brood per year. First flight: about 50 days.
VOCAL CALL	Series of 3–8 loud, low hoots. Second and third notes sometimes short and stacatto.

LONG-EARED OWL

RANGE

Approximate normal range of species.

States where species is occasionally sighted.

VITAL STATISTICS

NAME	**Long-eared owl** *Asio otus* FRENCH CANADIAN hibou à oreilles longues SPANISH búho-cornudo caricafé
DESCRIPTION	Medium to large size. Elongated body shape. Large ear tufts. Bill dark in color; eyes with yellow pigment. Body brown and grayish-brown with dark markings; chest and belly lighter with dark streaks and markings; face reddish-brown with dark border. Females darker and larger than males.
COMPARISON	Similar in coloring to great horned owl but smaller and with lankier body.

TOTAL LENGTH	13–16" 33–40.6 cm	**WING LENGTH**	11–12" 27.9–30.5 cm
WEIGHT	6½–12 oz 178–342 gms	**TAIL LENGTH**	4¾–6¼" 12.1–15.9 cm

RANGE	Permanent range throughout central and northern states, from Atlantic coast to Pacific coast, south to Mexico and upper southern states, north to lower British Columbia and extreme eastern provinces.
HABITAT	Forests, swamps. Hardwood and conifers.
HABITS	Nocturnal. May form nesting colonies during winter months. 3–8 eggs; incubated by female for about 21–30 days; male feeds female during incubation. First flight: 30–40 days.
VOCAL CALL	Usually quiet. Calls are single extended note, "hooooo."

NORTHERN HAWK OWL

RANGE

Approximate normal range of species.

● States where species is occasionally sighted.

Approximate winter range.

VITAL STATISTICS

NAME	**Northern hawk owl** *Surnia ulula* Canadian owl, falcon owl FRENCH CANADIAN chouette épervière
DESCRIPTION	Medium size. No ear tufts. Long tail. Bill pale yellow in color; eyes with yellow pigment. Body dark brown with light markings; chest and belly white with dark barring; face white with dark border. Females larger than males.
COMPARISON	Distinct hawk-like perching posture.

TOTAL LENGTH	14–17" 35.6–43.2 cm	**WING LENGTH**	8½–9½" 21.6–24.1 cm
WEIGHT	9–14 oz 273–392 gms	**TAIL LENGTH**	2¼–7" 5.7–17.8 cm

RANGE	Coast to coast in Canada, including Alaska, south to extreme northern Rocky Mountains and extreme northern Great Lakes states.
HABITAT	Conifer forests. Prefers semi-cleared and fringe areas with clearings.
HABITS	Diurnal. 3–7 eggs; incubation by females in 25–30 days; males feed females during incubation. First flight: 25–35 days.
VOCAL CALL	Series of short, rapid notes "ki, ki, ki, ki."

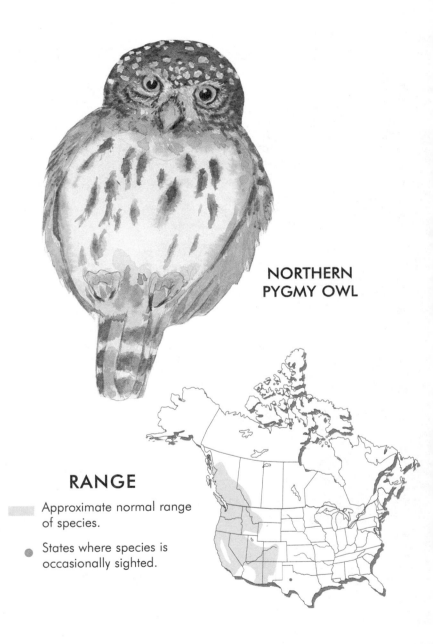

**NORTHERN
PYGMY OWL**

RANGE

Approximate normal range
of species.

States where species is
occasionally sighted.

VITAL STATISTICS

NAME	**Northern pygmy owl** *Glaucidium gnoma* FRENCH CANADIAN chouette pygmée SPANISH tecolotito serrano
DESCRIPTION	Small size. Boxy shape. No ear tufts. Long tail. Bill pale in color; eyes with yellow pigment. Two color phases: body reddish brown and body gray to grayish-brown. Lower chest and belly white with dark streaking. Distinctive dark eye-like markings on back of head. Females larger than males.
COMPARISON	Similar to ferruginous pygmy owl in size but northern pygmy owl has distinctive long, narrow tail.

TOTAL LENGTH	6–7½" 15.2–19.1 cm	**WING LENGTH**	3¼–4" 8.3–10.2 cm
WEIGHT	2–3 oz 54–87 gms	**TAIL LENGTH**	2¼–2½" 5.7–6.4 cm

RANGE	Western Mexico, U.S., and Canada, from Pacific coast east through Rocky Mountains.
HABITAT	Forests, mountains, foothills, canyons, typically from 5,000–10,000 feet. Conifer and conifer-hardwoods.
HABITS	Diurnal. Often hunts in early and late daylight hours. Sometimes caches food. 3–4 eggs; incubated by female; unknown incubation period. 1 brood per year. Unknown time of first flight.
VOCAL CALL	Single or double whistle-like note "whooo."

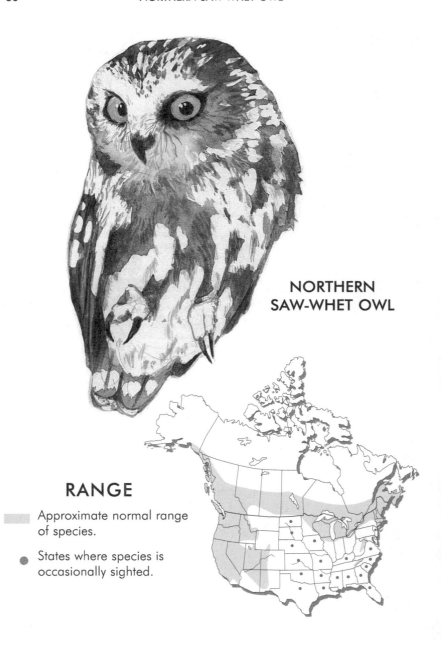

NORTHERN SAW-WHET OWL

RANGE

Approximate normal range of species.

States where species is occasionally sighted.

VITAL STATISTICS

NAME	**Northern saw-whet owl** *Aegolius acadicus* Acadian owl **FRENCH CANADIAN** chouette des granges **SPANISH** tecolote-abetero norteño
DESCRIPTION	Small size. Wide head and body shape. No ear tufts. Bill dark in color; eyes with yellow pigment. Body reddish-brown; chest and belly reddish-brown; face brown to reddish-brown with central white patch. Females slightly larger than males.
COMPARISON	Smallest owl in eastern North America.

TOTAL LENGTH	7–8½" 17.8–21.6 cm	**WING LENGTH**	5¼–5¾" 13.3–14.6 cm
WEIGHT	2–4 oz 54–124 gms	**TAIL LENGTH**	2½–3" 6.4–7.6 cm

RANGE	Throughout lower 48 states from Pacific coast to Atlantic coast, northern Mexico north to lower Canada, along Pacific coast north to Alaska.
HABITAT	Forests, swamps. Dense conifers and mixed conifer-hardwoods.
HABITS	Nocturnal. 4–7 eggs; incubated mostly by female for 21–28 days. First flight: 27–34 days.
VOCAL CALL	Distinctive series of raspy notes like saw being sharpened, also repeated single whistle.

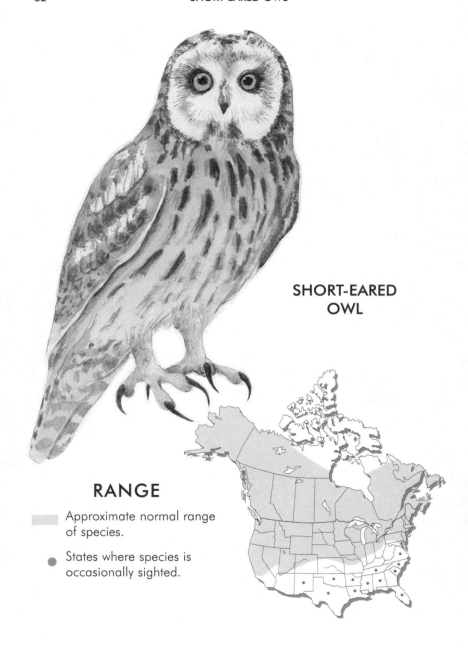

**SHORT-EARED
OWL**

RANGE

Approximate normal range
of species.

● States where species is
occasionally sighted.

VITAL STATISTICS

NAME	**Short-eared owl** *Asio flammeus* marsh owl, swamp owl **FRENCH CANADIAN** hibou à oreilles courtes **SPANISH** búho orejicorto
DESCRIPTION	Medium size. Ear tufts small or not noticeable. Bill dark in color with pale tip; eyes with yellow pigment. Body light brown to tawny with bold markings; chest and belly white to light brown with bold dark markings. Females and males about same size; females often darker in color.
COMPARISON	Similar in size and shape to long-eared owl, but paler in color and usually more visible in day.

TOTAL LENGTH	13–17" 33–43.2 cm	**WING LENGTH**	11½–12¾" 29.2–32.4 cm
WEIGHT	7–17 oz 206–475 gms	**TAIL LENGTH**	5¼–6½" 13.3–16.5 cm

RANGE	Permanent throughout central region of U.S. from Pacific coast to Atlantic coast, north into lower Canada. Breeding range north throughout Canada and Alaska.
HABITAT	Prairies, marshes, tundra; also open fields, brush, and clearings.
HABITS	Diurnal. Often hunts in early and late daylight hours. Nests on ground. 4–9 eggs; incubated mostly by female for about 21–29 days. First flight: 24–27 days. May live in loose colonies.
VOCAL CALL	Series of raspy, high-pitched notes.

SNOWY OWL

RANGE

Approximate normal range of species.

● States where species is occasionally sighted.

Approximate winter range.

VITAL STATISTICS

NAME	**Snowy owl** *Nyctea scandiaca* arctic owl, ghost owl, ermine owl FRENCH CANADIAN hibou blanc
DESCRIPTION	Large size. No ear tufts. Bill dark in color; eyes with yellow pigment. Body white with sparse light brown and darker markings. Females are larger and have more and darker markings than males.
COMPARISON	Only large owl with white plumage.

TOTAL LENGTH	20–28" 50.8–71.1 cm	**WING LENGTH**	15½–18" 39.4–45.7 cm
WEIGHT	3–6 lbs 1320–2690 gms	**TAIL LENGTH**	8½–10¾" 21.6–27.3 cm

RANGE	Permanent in extreme northern Canada and Alaska. Migratory in winter south to upper Great Lakes states, northern plains states, and northwest. Occasional winter visitor south to central California and upper region of southern states.
HABITAT	Tundra.
HABITS	Diurnal. Hunts mostly during day in summer. Nests on ground. 5–7 eggs; females incubate eggs for 27–38 days; males feed females during incubation. First flight: about 30–50 days.
VOCAL CALL	Mostly silent. Main call is short series of long, deep-pitched "hoooo, hooooo, hoooo."

SPOTTED OWL

RANGE

Approximate normal range
of species.

VITAL STATISTICS

NAME	**Spotted owl** *Strix occidentalis* Xántus owl, wood owl FRENCH CANADIAN chat-huant tacheté SPANISH búho manchado
DESCRIPTION	Medium to large size. No ear tufts. Bill pale in color; dark eyes with no yellow pigment. Body brown with white spots; chest and belly brown with white streaks and spots. Females larger than males.
COMPARISON	Similar to barred owl, but markings are white rather than dark and white spots distinctive to spotted owl.

TOTAL LENGTH	16–19" 40.6–48.3 cm	**WING LENGTH**	12–12¾" 30.5–32.4 cm
WEIGHT	1–1¾ lbs 518–760 gms	**TAIL LENGTH**	8–8¾" 20.3–22.2 cm

RANGE	Permanent along extreme Pacific coast, California to British Columbia, central Sierras, and parts of central Arizona and New Mexico.
HABITAT	Dense forests, canyons. Prefers conifers.
HABITS	Nocturnal. 2–3 eggs; incubation by females in 28–32 days. First flight: 40–45 days.
VOCAL CALL	3–4 short, barking notes.

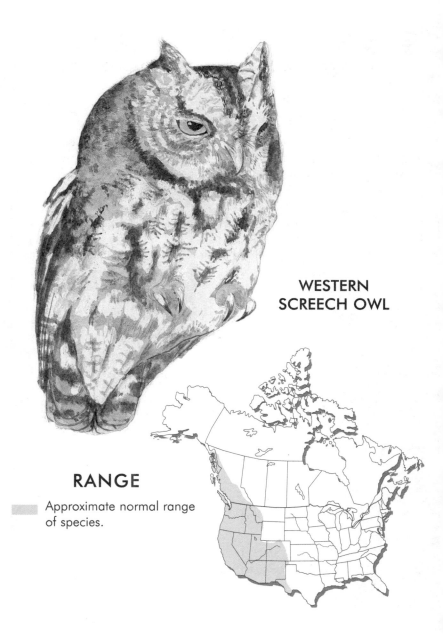

WESTERN
SCREECH OWL

RANGE

Approximate normal range
of species.

VITAL STATISTICS

NAME	**Western screech owl** *Otus kennicotti* little horned owl, duck owl SPANISH tecolote occidental
DESCRIPTION	Small owl. Bill black in color; eyes with yellow pigment. Ear tufts prominent when raised. Body overall gray to brownish-gray in color; chest and belly barred. Females and males the same size.
COMPARISON	Similar to whiskered screech owl, but with black bill.

TOTAL LENGTH	6½–8" 16.5–20.3 cm	**WING LENGTH**	6½–7½" 16.5–19.1 cm
WEIGHT	2½–4½ oz 140–236 gms	**TAIL LENGTH**	3¼–4" 8.3–10.2 cm

RANGE	In Canada, throughout Pacific coast mountain ranges. In U.S., throughout Pacific coast east through Rocky Mountains.
HABITAT	Open woodlands, desert, wooded stream and river banks.
HABITS	Nocturnal. 2–7 eggs; incubated mostly by female for 21–30 days; males feed females during incubation. Females and males mate for life. First flight: not known.
VOCAL CALL	Series of short whistles with increasing tempo at end. Also double trilled tone, with second trill longer.

**WHISKERED
SCREECH OWL**

RANGE

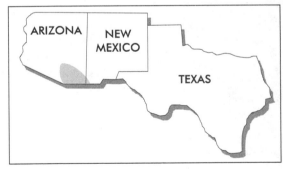

Approximate
normal range
of species.

ARIZONA   NEW
           MEXICO

                        TEXAS

VITAL STATISTICS

NAME	**Whiskered screech owl** *Otus trichopsis* spotted screech owl SPANISH tecolote bigotudo
DESCRIPTION	One of the smallest owls. Bill pale in color; eyes with yellow pigment. Ear tufts noticeable when raised. Prominent, irregular barring on chest. Females slightly larger than males.
COMPARISON	Similar to western screech owl, but western screech owl is about 10 percent larger and has less prominent whisker markings on face.

TOTAL LENGTH	7" 17.8 cm	WING LENGTH	5½–6" 13.9–15.2 cm
WEIGHT	2½–4¼ oz 70–121 gm	**TAIL LENGTH**	2½–3" 6.4–7.6 cm

RANGE	Limited areas in extreme southern Arizona south through central Mexico.
HABITAT	Dense forests at 4,000–6,500 feet elevation. Oak, conifers, oak-conifer woods.
HABITS	Nocturnal. 3–4 eggs; no information available about incubation or fledging.
VOCAL CALL	Short whistling tones at an even pitch; irregular series of staccato hoots.

EVOLUTION

"The dancing owl waves his spread tail feathers.
I'm the owl.
The dancing owl waves his spread tail feathers.
I'm the owl.
I now tell you by my dancing, I'm the owl.
The dancing owl waves his spread tail feathers.
I'm the owl."   — Baluba rhyme from the Congo, Africa

The oldest known owl fossils come from the lower Miocene era, roughly 38–54 million years ago. These early owls eventually evolved into the two families that today comprise the order, the typical owls and the barn owls. Fossil records show that the earliest known barn owls date to about 24 million years ago, suggesting that they may have diverged from an earlier ancestor common to both modern owl families.

During the upper Pleistocene, about 30,000 years ago, giant barn owls once thrived in what is now Cuba. This ancient owl was two to three times as large as modern barn owls — up to an estimated three feet in length. Known as *ornimegalonyx*, these birds were the largest owls that ever lived, twice the size of great horned owls. When this giant bird was alive, about 10,000 years ago, it would have preyed upon animals such as the giant sloth and huge rodents that were as big as modern pigs. Fossil evidence of these birds has been found in Cuba and other islands in the Caribbean and Mediterranean regions. Scientists speculate that the widespread existence of these large flying predators — along with giant eagles, hawks, and vultures — may have resulted because there were no mammalian predators on these islands. And because of their size and their relatively small wings, it is possible they may have flown very little, if at all.

In the world today, there are 134 species of owls, spread through-

SCIENTIFIC CLASSIFICATION

KINGDOM	•	Animals
PHYLUM	•	Chordata (vertebrates)
CLASS	•	Aves (birds)
ORDER	•	Strigiforme (owls)
FAMILY	•	Strigoides
GENUS	•	Strix
SPECIES	•	varia (barred owl)

out all continents and even on many isolated islands. (Note: The total number of species is subject to change, as biologists continually reexamine the classification of existing specimens.) The largest owl in the world is the eagle owl, found in parts of Europe and Asia; the smallest is the elf owl, found only in North America.

Although the owl species of the world share many similar characteristics, they are not all the same. About two-thirds of the world's owls, for example, are active at night, the rest either hunt only during the day or are active during both periods (but not in the same twenty-four hour period!). Not all owls are silent fliers, either. A few, such as the elf owl, lack the soft extensions on feathers that muffle the sound of air during flight. Owls in some regions are more migratory than those in North America, following regular seasonal routes from one region to another. Of all the world's owls, barn owls are the most common. With more than thirty species in this family, barn owls are found on almost every continent.

WORLD BIRDS

ORDER	DESCRIPTION	No. of SPECIES	No. of FAMILIES
STRUTHIONIFORMES	ostriches	1	1
RHEIFORMES	rheas	2	1
CASUARIIFORMES	cassowaries, emus	4	2
APTERYGIFORMES	kiwis	3	1
TINAMIFORMES	tinamous	45	1
SPHENISCIFORMES	penguins	16	1
GAVIFORMES	loons	4	1
PODICIPEDIFORMES	grebes	20	1
PROCELLARIIFORMES	albatross, petrels	93	4
PELECANIFORMES	pelicans, gannets, cormorants	57	6
CICONIIFORMES	herons, storks, flamingos	115	6
ANSERIFORMES	ducks, geese, swans	150	2
FALCONIFORMES	vultures, eagles, hawks	286	5
GALLIFORMES	grouse, turkeys, quail	256	6
GRUIFORMES	cranes, limpkins, sunbitterns	197	12
CHARADRIIFORMES	auks, snipes, plovers, gulls	319	17
COLUMBIFORMES	pigeons, doves	316	2
PSITTACIFORMES	parrots, macaws, lovebirds	330	1
CUCULIFORMES	turacos, cuckoos, roadrunners	151	3
STRIGIFORMES	owls	134	2
CAPRIMULGIFORMES	oilbirds, nightjars	96	5
APODIFORMES	hummingbirds, swifts	403	3
COLIIFORMES	mousebirds	6	1
TROGONIFORMES	trogons	35	1
CORACIIFORMES	kingfishers, hornbills	193	9
PICIFORMES	toucans, woodpeckers, barbets	376	6
PASSERIFORMES	larks, wrens, dippers, starlings, orioles, crows, tanagers, finches	5219	63

NORTH AMERICAN OWL SUBSPECIES

SPECIES	NUMBER OF SUBSPECIES
BARN OWL	1 in North America (36 total)
BARRED OWL	3 in North America (4 total)
BOREAL OWL	1 in North America (2 total)
BURROWING OWL	2 in North America (19 total)
EASTERN SCREECH OWL	5 in North America
ELF OWL	2 in North America (4 total)
FERRUGINOUS PYGMY OWL	1 in North America (11 total)
FLAMMULATED OWL	1 in North America (6 total)
GREAT GRAY OWL	1 in North America (3 total)
GREAT HORNED OWL	10 in North America (17 total)
LONG-EARED OWL	2 in North America (4 total)
NORTHERN HAWK OWL	1 in North America (8 total)
NORTHERN PYGMY OWL	4 in North America (7 total)
NORTHERN SAW-WHET OWL	2 in North America
SHORT-EARED OWL	1 in North America (10 total)
SNOWY OWL	No subspecies
SPOTTED OWL	3 in North America
WESTERN SCREECH OWL	5 in North America (8 total)
WHISKERED SCREECH OWL	1 in North America (3 total)

MALAYSIAN EAGLE OWL

EURASIAN EAGLE OWL

SPOTTED LITTLE
OWL

WHITE-FACED
SCOPS OWL

AFRICAN WOOD
OWL

WORLD OWLS

OWL ANATOMY

"Such persons as conclude, when looking upon Owls in the glare of day, that they are, as they then appear, extremely dull, are greatly mistaken."

— John James Audubon (*Birds of America*, 1840)

Owls, unlike most other birds, are remarkably similar in appearance when comparing males and females of the same species. Coloring, patterns, and body size are about the same for most owl species in North America, although size differences are more apparent in the larger species. Male and female pygmy owls, for example, look virtually identical while great horned owls vary in size by as much as 25 percent.

Why have most owl species evolved to produce larger females? Studies of owl prey indicate males and females of the same species, even mating pairs, generally attack, kill, and eat the same size prey, therefore the larger size of females is unlikely to have developed because of differences in diet, a common factor in other animal species where one sex is larger than the other. Females may need an advantage in size in order to successfully incubate and brood, but here, also, other bird species do not show the same development. One intriguing possibility about this discrepancy in owl size relates to the aggressive, predatory nature of this animal. Owls often attack other predatory birds, even those as large as itself. Therefore, female owls may have evolved to be larger than males in order to reduce the potential of attack by males.

Owl species vary in both size and shape and some of this variation may be an efficient adaptation for how they hunt and their preferred hunting habitat. Owls that seek out prey while soaring over open territory, for instance, typically have large, slender wings. Owls that maneuver through forests in search of prey are often smaller and have shorter, broader wings. But all owls have powerful

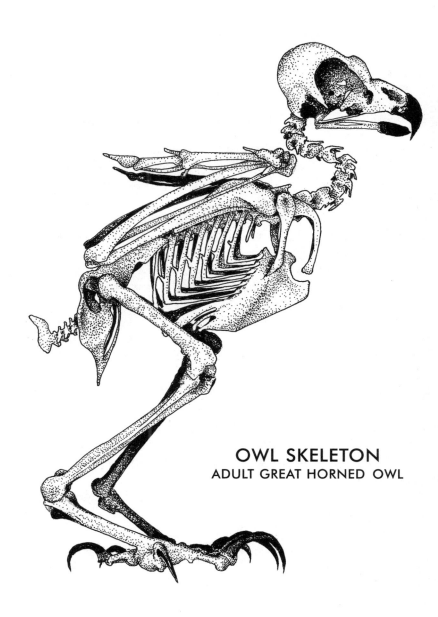

OWL SKELETON
ADULT GREAT HORNED OWL

OWL SKULL
ADULT GREAT HORNED OWL

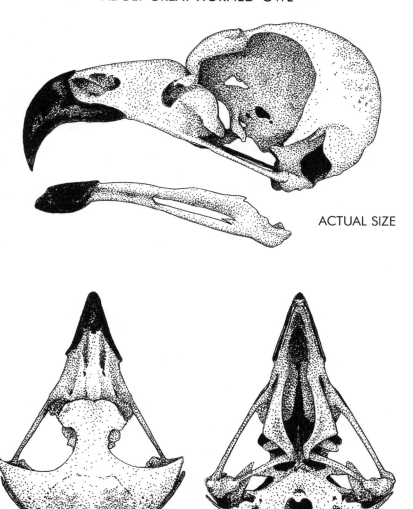

ACTUAL SIZE

flying capabilities because their wings are relatively large compared to their body size and their bodies are relatively light in weight. Like all birds, owl skeletons provide strength without excessive weight, a feature gained because of a unique bone structure that is mostly air space. Owl skeletons consist of 7 to 9 percent of their total weight, similar to other birds.

Most owls have remarkably small bodies; most of their size comes from their feathers. The relatively large mass of feathers on such small bodies is one adaptation that allows them to withstand severely cold weather without much body fat for protection. And even though their metabolisms are fairly rapid, the small body size means that in most cases, they do not have to be continually eating in order to produce enough energy to survive.

Owls exhibit a variety of flying styles. Some soar more than others and a few species rarely take more than short flights. The great gray owl is noted for its slow, steady wing style. The short eared owl, on the other hand, is often observed flitting along the ground in short, arcing patterns.

Owls are built more for lift than speed. Their wings are larger in proportion to their body size than most birds — along with a skeleton that is extremely lightweight — and give these birds the ability to carry prey animals through the air.

A few owl species can hover in the air for brief periods of time, a tactic helpful when hunting small rodents close to the ground. But the hummingbird is the only bird that can perform true hovering flight; when owls hover they must face into a wind and equalize their forward flight with this force of air.

COLOR AND PATTERN

When observing a collection of North American owls, many observers are struck by the remarkable similarities in colors and patterns among the species. This order of birds seems drab, monotonously gray and brown, and lacking in the bright plumage and feathery displays found in many other groups of birds, even considering the snowy owl, which can be almost completely white. But it is just this similarity and palette of drab colors that give owls one of their most distinctive features, the ability to blend in with their surroundings.

Variation in owl colors and patterns are significant, even if lacking in wide range. The marking characteristics on each species gen-

The colors and patterns on owl feathers give them an enhanced ability to blend in with their surroundings. Variations in grays and browns among species are closely linked to the dominant trees in the habitats they favor.

Even the plumage of the largest owls, which are not threatened by many predators, allows them to hide from danger.

When threatened, many owls take up a unique "cryptic" posture, raising their ear tufts, closing their eyes, and condensing their feathers.

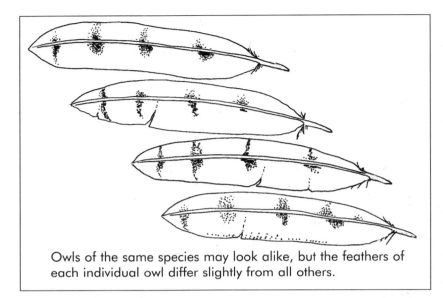

Owls of the same species may look alike, but the feathers of each individual owl differ slightly from all others.

erally corresponds with the predominant vegetation in their home range. Owls such as the eastern screech owl, which have two color phases, exhibit this feature even more. In the northern part of their range, for example, the most common color phase is gray, an efficient blend with the bark of hardwood trees most often found there. In the southern part of their range, the red color phase is most common, matching the reddish bark color of pine trees, a widespread tree throughout the southern part of the owl's range.

Coloring in owls provides tremendously effective camouflage. Although they are not often threatened by predators, their mostly nocturnal habits puts them at the greatest risk when they are resting, in broad daylight. This is when coloration serves them best, blending into branches, foliage, and bark and imitating natural shadows. The hashed, barred, and spotted patterns on their feathers efficiently mask their bodies, extending the existing shadows of their normal perching sites into a continuous image. Their large eyes, a major identifying feature, can also be masked. When closed,

CLEANING

Feathers collect dust, grime, and parasites. In response, owls frequently groom and clean their feathers to keep them in good working order. Like most birds, owls use their bills and talons to carefully scrape material from the feathers. A more important use of the bill on feathers is not for cleaning, but feather repair. Flight feathers on owls — as on all flying birds — have a structure of barb and barbules that form a uniform, effective surface with an interlocking mesh. This mesh is frequently "unhooked" during harsh flying conditions or impacts with objects or prey. While preening, an owl uses its bill to delicately realign the unhooked

Barn owl using its bill to preen primary flight feathers.

barbs. A small gland called the uropygial gland produces a thin oily liquid that provides a protective coating on the feathers. This gland, located at the base of the tail, is stimulated with the bill, which is used to transfer the coating to the feathers. Owls may also take an occasional bath, splashing in the shallow water of puddles or streams. Some owl preening is not so much for cleaning as bonding. Mated pairs of owls in some species engage in mutual preening, an activity that helps keep their feathers clean but also strengthens and reinforces their relationship.

the eyelids on most owls feature patterns and bands of colors that complete the overall camouflage effect found on the rest of their heads. In fact, the most recognizable feature about owls to their prey — mostly smaller birds — is not their color but their shape. The silhouette of an owl is instantly recognizable and often triggers a mobbing attack.

Some of their camouflage may also be linked to owl behavior patterns. When threatened by intruders, owls of many species initially respond by freezing, not flight. In these circumstances, owls typically assume a "cryptic posture," elongating their bodies, pulling in their feathers to minimize identity, raising their ear tufts, and closing their eyes. In this way, they create the best effect for blending into their immediate environment.

Another significant feature of owl coloring is their unique facial features. With very large eyes and generally large heads, owl faces are made even more distinctive by accents, lines, and color variations that can magnify their facial features. Possibly developed as a means of effective communication with other owls, they can use these features effectively. By spreading or flattening facial feathers, they can make their eyes appear larger — and presumably more threatening — or smaller; raising or lowering their ear tufts may also be used as a visual signal. Special feathers around the bill are also manipulable.

The snowy owl, distinctly unmarked compared to other species in North America, also derives camouflage benefit from its coloring. From the ground or air, a female in her nest blends into the surrounding terrain because during the nesting season for snowy owls, some or all of the ground is still covered with snow.

FEATHERS

Owl feathers, like those of most birds, include two major types, contour feathers and down feathers. Unlike most birds, however, down feathers are relatively scarce on owls. Soft and fluffy, down serves to trap air and create a layer of insulation next to a bird's body. Owls do not suffer from a lack of down, however, because of the insulation value they get from special downy barbules on the lower portions of the contour feathers.

Specialized feather designs appear in different places on the owl's body. Around the face, feather varieties include the crown, ruff, facial disk, ear flap, and those around the bill. Feathery tendrils around the feet form a type of early warning system. They work like feelers to help owls react to things they touch, especially prey animals.

One special feather adaptation makes owls different from all other birds. The primary feathers on the wings, responsible for lifting and carrying them

At the front edge of the flight feathers, the feather barbs are loose and unattached, creating a soft surface that diffuses the rush of air during flight.

through the air, have unique adaptations on the leading edge. There, soft surfaces perform an important function, filtering the shock of air as it flows over the surface of the wing during flight. This functions effectively as a muffler, reducing the usual sound of rushing air into near silence. This soft surface is an adaptation of a structure found on all feathers — the individual barbs that radiate from the central shaft. Only a few species of owls, those that typically hunt during the day, lack this adaptation.

On the flight feathers of an owl, barbs along the front edge of the feather are loose and unattached to one another, at least for the outer section. On all other flight feathers — including those on all other birds — the barbs, which run parallel to one another, are hooked together by barbules and barbicels, tiny extensions that overlap and hook together, forming a flexible surface.

On other parts of an owl's body, some contour feathers also feature barbules that have been adapted into long, soft plumes. This adaptation also helps muffle the sound of air rushing by in flight.

Even without a thick coating of down, owl feathers provide efficient insulation from extremes of weather. Cold temperatures are no problem to the snowy owl, for instance, because its feathers are an effective barrier. This effect comes from a high percentage of air cells trapped within the feather structures. The feathers of the snowy owl are even more insulating than other owls and have been measured as the second most effective insulating feathers of all birds, exceeded only by feathers of the Adelie penguin in their ability to slow the escape of heat from the body. Snowy owl feathers are also just as effective as the most efficient mammal fur in providing insulation; they have been measured as equivalent in insulation value to the thickest furs of hardy animals such as the arctic fox.

Owls have some degree of control over their feathers, being able to flex portions of their skin in such a way as to expand or condense their plumage against their bodies. To appear larger, they may fluff up their feathers. To escape detection, they can also flatten their feathers, reducing their silhouettes and improving the camouflage effect of the plumage.

FEET AND TALONS

Owl feet have four toes. In flight, three point forward and one points to the rear, but when perching, most often a bird will have two pointing forward and two to the rear. When they strike and clutch their prey, owls also use the two-and-two pattern. This provides the most efficient clutching ability, a natural technique that is made even more practical by a locking mechanism in the muscles and ligaments that control the toes and talons. When the back toes are brought forward around a perch or prey animal, the talons grip with an overwhelming force. Owls are able to use both patterns with their toes because one, the outer toe, has a unique flexible joint that allows it to be swiveled through a wide range.

On the barn owl, but not other owl species, the feet have a middle toe that features a web-like extension. Like a barber's comb, this toe is used to groom its feathers. But the other owl species, even without this special feature, still make good use of their talons when preening.

Talons on owls are their principal means of gathering food. As such, they have evolved into strong, sharp instruments that are capable of piercing tough animal skin and holding heavy weights. The bony structures in owl feet are also adapted to help in this task, being shorter and stronger than similar bones in other birds so as to better withstand the force of impact made by an owl hurtling into its prey. Talons on female owls are typically longer and heavier than on males.

Some species have short, stubby talons and others feature longer, thinner units, but the claws are uniformly very sharp on the tips. The color of talons also varies among species, from very dark, almost black, to pale gray or ivory in tone.

Talons on most owls can be spread wide, increasing their striking and gripping capabilities. Some studies have shown a direct relationship between the distance of the spread in a single species and the size of the animals it preys upon most.

The underside of an owl's foot has no feathers but is covered with a rough, nobby surface that helps it grip when perching or holding prey. The entire surface of the top of the foot is covered in feathers, except for the talons. Most of the

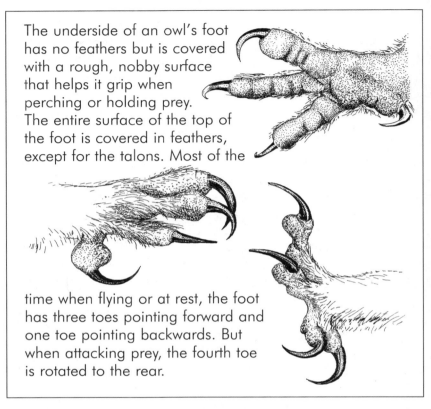

time when flying or at rest, the foot has three toes pointing forward and one toe pointing backwards. But when attacking prey, the fourth toe is rotated to the rear.

Except for burrowing owls, the feet of North American owls are covered with feathers, a protection against cold temperatures. Depending on the species, the feathers may be long or short but the the base of the foot is always bare. To avoid overheating in hot weather, some owl species can help regulate their body temperatures with their feet. Excess body heat is radiated away through the soles of their feet, which are supplied with extra blood vessels.

As the principal tool with which owls strike and hold their prey, feet and talons have evolved to be very effective weapons. Strength tests given to measure the gripping power of talons show owls to be among the strongest birds in this category. Stories of humans who unfortunately become entangled with large owls confirm this remarkable strength. In one case, a biologist gripped by a great horned owl could not be freed from the clutches of the owl until the owl's leg tendons were severed, releasing the talons.

BILLS

All owls feature the same general type of bill, a short, curved beak well-designed for gripping and stripping prey. The exposed part of the bill is covered with a hard, durable horny surface. The lower edge of the upper bill and the upper edge of the lower bill taper to a sharp edge and overlap with one another; the two surfaces work like a pair of scissors, able to snip through tough tissue.

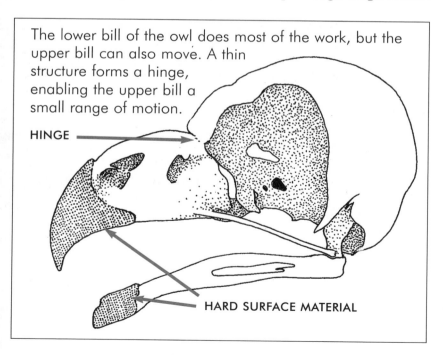

The lower bill of the owl does most of the work, but the upper bill can also move. A thin structure forms a hinge, enabling the upper bill a small range of motion.

HINGE

HARD SURFACE MATERIAL

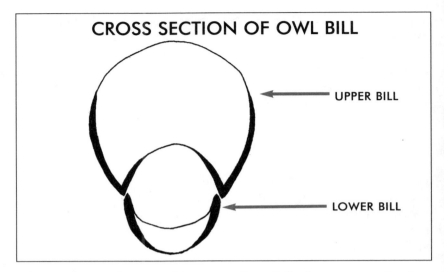

CROSS SECTION OF OWL BILL

UPPER BILL

LOWER BILL

The smallest owls in North America have bills that are one-third to one-half inch in length. Great gray owls and great horned owls are at the other extreme; their beaks can be up to two inches in length.

The lower bill does most of the work for the owl but the upper bill is also capable of moving. At the back of the bill, where it joins the skull, a narrow strip of flexible tissue acts like a hinge, allowing the bill to swivel up a short distance. Other raptors and bird species also have this structural feature, which may also be used in some kinds of visual communications.

When overheated, some owls "pant" through partially-opened bills in order to reduce their body temperature.

OWL SIGHT

"What if you could witness with owls' eyes the revelry of the wood mice some night, frisking about the wood like so many little kangaroos?"
— Henry David Thoreau (*Journal*, January 4, 1860)

Some biologists believe that of all birds, owls have the best eyesight under low-light conditions. Comparing owl anatomy to other birds, this is not surprising, given the huge size of their eyes in relation to the size of their heads. With the size comes added weight. Dr. Paul Johnsgard, a noted ornithologist, has determined that for owls, the weight of the eyes is 1 to 5 percent of their body weight, the same ratio found in humans for the weight of the brain to the body. In some of the larger species, owl eyes are larger than their brains and weigh about the same as those in a large male human.

Large eyes contain more and better defined optical structures for analyzing light, but as owl eyes have evolved to achieve this great ability, they have pushed the limits of what their skulls can do to hold these orbs. The result is a pair of eyeballs that having reached a maximum size and pushed out of the traditional spherical shape for animal eyes; owl eyes are more like elongated tubes. Not being spherical, the eyes do not easily roll inside their sockets and are, in effect, fixed to the skull. Not being able to move their eyes, owls must move their entire heads to change their field of view. The eyes themselves are held within special structures called sclerotic rings. These rings are found in all birds, but in the owl, they have evolved to be larger than in other birds. Unlike other soft tissue, the sclerotic rings are not usually attacked by beetles and other scavengers after an owl dies; an owl skull found in the wild will often include these rings still attached to the eye sockets.

Owl heads have an unusual degree of rotation to make up for

their lack of eyeball movement. With extremely flexible necks — fourteen neck bones and a swiveling bone structure at the base of the neck — they can turn their heads almost completely around. Their total range of head motion is up to 270 degrees in either direction for most species, permitting them to look directly to the rear without turning their bodies. The field of view, however, is somewhat limited, about 110 degrees, with a little more than half of that arc, about 70 degrees, providing binocular vision. By comparison, human eyesight covers about 180 degrees, with about 140 degrees comprised of binocular vision.

Owls eyes, in order to work well at night, require great efficiency in gathering and processing light. This efficiency comes primarily from a large pupil and cornea, the equivalent of a camera lens in the process of light collection. Compared to the human eye, an owl

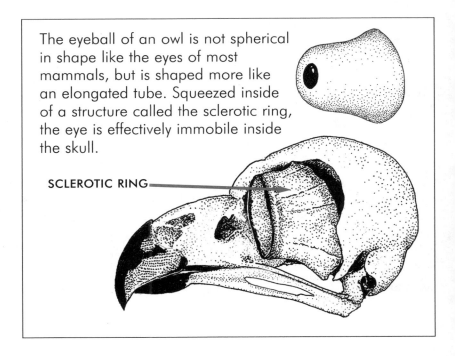

The eyeball of an owl is not spherical in shape like the eyes of most mammals, but is shaped more like an elongated tube. Squeezed inside of a structure called the sclerotic ring, the eye is effectively immobile inside the skull.

SCLEROTIC RING

Owls have remarkably flexible necks. They can rotate their heads about 270 degrees, a necessary function when spotting or tracking prey, because their eyes cannot move in their heads. Owls may also turn their heads almost completely upside down. They do this in reaction to something that is spotted high in their field of vision. The sharpest zone in an owl's field of vision is directly in front of its eyes but below normal eye level; by turning its head upside down, the owl can focus most clearly on what is above it.

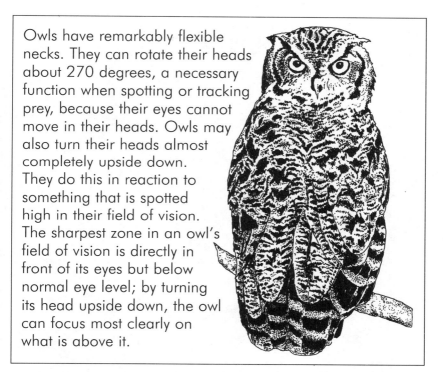

eye is up to three times as efficient in the task of processing light. Among owl species, this ability varies somewhat, with the burrowing owl last in ability; burrowing owls are estimated to have about the same ability to see in dim light as humans. But for the other owls, light gathering capability has developed further than anywhere else in the animal kingdom. The only mammal that comes close to the owl in its ability to see in dim conditions is the cat.

Although they may excel in the dark, owls are not blind in bright sunlight, as some myths have described. All owls are capable of normal daytime vision. In both night and daytime lighting, they are deficient in detecting color, seeing most objects in degrees of black and white.

More so than in most other animals, owl eyes react to the amount of light that is available. The iris can expand to fill almost the entire cornea in the darkest conditions, permitting the maximum amount of light to be recorded at the back of the eye.

Upper and lower eyelids (top) close during rest. A third eyelid, called the nictating membrane (bottom), closes diagonally across the eye to clean or protect the surface.

Many animals that are nocturnal and have increased vision under low light conditions feature an effect called "eyeshine." If an artificial source of light, such as a flashlight, hits one of these types of eyes when it is in the dark, it will appear to glow, usually orange or red. At night, when owls are exposed to a source of light, their eyes will exhibit varying degrees of eyeshine, with colors from red to gold.

Owl eyes come equipped with a nictating membrane, a thin layer of tissue that flicks across the eye — from the inside corner diagonally to the outside corner — to protect it and keep it clean and moist. But this and their tremendous powers of vision in the dark are not enough to guarantee their safety. Many owls are injured, sometimes fatally, by flying into or against obstructions while they are hunting. Some owls also receive injuries to their eyes from hitting obstructions while they are hunting.

In addition to the nictating membrane, owls have eyelids, both upper and lower. The upper eyelids are used in blinking movements, which help clean the eyes. The lower eyelids are pulled up over the eyes during sleep.

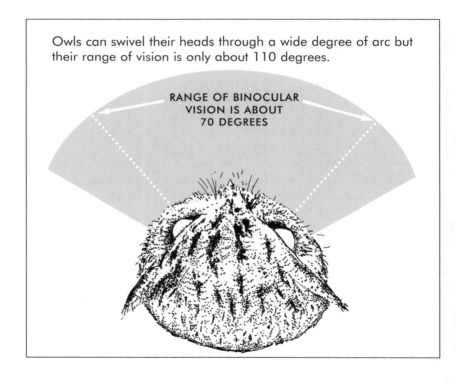

Owls can swivel their heads through a wide degree of arc but their range of vision is only about 110 degrees.

RANGE OF BINOCULAR VISION IS ABOUT 70 DEGREES

OWL HEARING

"How often, when snugly settled under the boughs of my temporary encampment, and preparing to roast a venison steak or the body of a squirrel, have I been saluted with the exulting bursts of this nightly disturber of the peace, that, had it not been for him, would have prevailed around me, as well as in my lonely retreat!"

— John James Audubon (*Birds of America,* 1840)

Owl ears are among the most unique in the animal kingdom. Not only do they function well in picking up the faintest sounds, their placement and construction gives owls a tremendous advantage in pinpointing distances and directions. The owl's head is one major component of this design system. The owl's face forms a shallow, elliptical depression with the ears at the edges. Facial feathers are typically stiff and reflective, helping capture, "steer," and amplify sound waves toward the ears, just like a parabolic dish antenna is used to capture television signals.

With the face turned toward a source of sound, the opposing ears are able to distinguish minute differences in the direction of the sound's origin. Ears locate sources along horizontal surfaces by comparing the level of sound between the left and right "channels." The closer an ear is to the sound source, the louder the sound appears. If both ears receive the same level, the sound comes from directly ahead of the owl. To pinpoint a horizontal direction of sound, the owl turns its head from side to side until the sounds are equalized.

Owl ears, unlike those of almost any other animal, including humans, can also perform another directional trick. In most owl species, the ears are not symmetrical, and this permits them extra precision in determining the height of a sound source. This asymmetrical design feature lies in the openings into the ear cavities. In

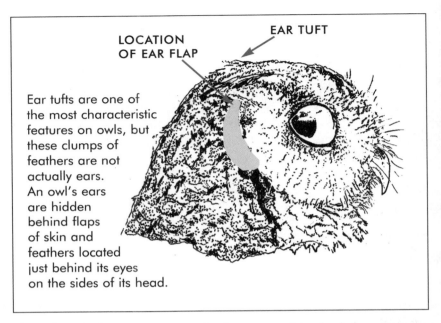

LOCATION OF EAR FLAP

EAR TUFT

Ear tufts are one of the most characteristic features on owls, but these clumps of feathers are not actually ears. An owl's ears are hidden behind flaps of skin and feathers located just behind its eyes on the sides of its head.

the right ear the opening is at the bottom and in the left ear it is at the top. The two offsetting ear openings allow the owl to hear differences in the height of a sound source the same way the separation of the ears determines left and right; the opening closest to the sound source receives a louder signal. A sound will appear louder in the right ear if it is coming from below, and louder in the left ear if it is coming from above. If the sound is equal, the source is level with both ears.

The translation of left and right signals with those from up and down is combined instantly in the brain to create a mental image of the space where the source of the sound is located. Even in complete darkness, some owls — notably the barn owl — have demonstrated their ability to accurately and repeatedly locate and strike within 1 to 2 degrees of a target, close enough to snatch the animal unfortunate enough to have made a noise. Observers have noted that when a perched owl first hears a sound that represents a potential meal, it will move its head from side to side and up and down until it appears to be staring directly at the sound source. Responding to the sound, the owl is essentially "equalizing" the sound signals in each ear; when the sound is the same from left and right as well as up and down, it must be looking directly at the source.

The placement of owl ears also helps them detect sounds coming from the rear. The ear openings, unlike many mammals, don't block sounds from any direction. Owl ears also include an ear flap, a small movable extension of skin that can help funnel sounds coming from a particular direction.

In general, owls with the largest ear structures — including the greatest amount of difference between the left and right ears — are those that are most likely to hunt at night. Owls with the smallest and most symmetrical ear structures are most likely to hunt during the day, when visual signals outweigh sound in importance. One exception is the elf owl, which has small, symmetrical ear structures but hunts almost entirely at night.

Because the ears are extraordinarily sensitive, it doesn't take much sound to attract an owl. Much of the noise generated by small rodents — a major source of food for most owl species — is created as they scurry through ground cover. Owls are capable of detecting even tiny muffled noises created as small rodents move through tunnels under a blanket of snow. Hearing sensitivity in some owls is as much as ten times greater than human hearing for some frequencies, but not all owl species have this same degree of talent.

The acuteness of owl hearing is created by a combination of their head structure, the feathers used in funneling sound, and their unique ears. Owls with missing or damaged facial feathers have diminished capabilities for locating prey in the dark. Similarly, owls with only one functional ear are essentially incapable of judging distances by sound, although they can still hunt successfully using vision.

Although the ears capture sound, an owl's brain must be able to process the sound effectively if their hearing systems are to work to the best advantage. Studies of owl brains, in fact, show that the section of the brain that corresponds with hearing, the medulla, is more complex than in other birds. For barn owls, a typical medulla is estimated to have at least 95,000 neurons, three times the number in a crow, a bird that is twice the size of this owl.

Owl ears are hidden under feathers. On some owl species, however, tufts of feathers that protrude from the top of the head give the appearance of ears, and are, in fact, referred to as "ear tufts." But these clumps of feathers are not connected to the actual ears, nor do they seem to be involved in the process of hearing. Ear tufts are a mystery. Theories about why they appear on some owls include possible usefulness as camouflage and as an aid in communication with other owls, but these theories are not proven and are not even well supported. Ear tufts appear on seven out of the nineteen species of owls in North America.

MOLTING

"With all the gloomy habits and ungracious tones of the Owl, there is nothing in this bird supernatural or mysterious, or more than that of a simple bird of prey, formed for feeding by night, like many other animals, and of reposing by day."

— Alexander Wilson (*American Ornithology,* 1840)

The characteristic colors and patterns that bedeck owls derive from mature feathers. These feathers, even when kept clean, suffer from the wear and tear common in a bird's life. Normal abrasion and flexing gradually wears away the surface of feathers, and encounters with hard or sharp objects can tear, bend, or rip off entire feathers. Even with their noted ability to see and avoid obstacles in very dark conditions, collisions do happen, and damaged feathers are a typical consequence.

When owls are first born, flight feathers are absent. Baby owls are covered with downy feathers, a protective covering that helps keep

When birds molt, new feathers grow to replace the ones that have fallen out. As the new feathers emerge from the bird's skin, they are tightly bound inside thin shafts of tissue. At this stage, the new feathers are called *pin feathers*. Soon after emerging, the shaft splits open, allowing the new feather to unfurl and grow to its final size.

them warm. As they grow in the nest, this down is gradually replaced with their first suit of feathers, a juvenile plumage that is similar to their parents, but often paler and with different markings. For barn owl chicks, the first down is replaced in about two weeks with a second coat of down; this plumage is longer and denser than the first.

The first adult plumage for owls begins appearing within their first few months of life. These feathers are critical for the young birds, because they will empower the animals with the ability to fly. In the nest, the onset of adult plumage also means that juvenile owls begin preening and flexing their wings, in preparation for their first flight.

Birds regularly replace their feathers in a process known as molting. Most birds molt at least once a year and owls are no exception. Molting can rob a bird of peak performance, but it usually coincides with a period when an owl is least likely to suffer from a lack of flying capability. Molting typically begins after the parent birds have raised a brood and the young birds have left the nest and are feeding on their own.

The molting period spans several months, up to three months in some cases. During this period, feathers are gradually shed over the entire body in a regular pattern. Because birds must continue to fly in order to obtain food, molting has evolved to reduce the impact of lost feathers at any given time in the molting period. Particularly with major flight feathers in the wings, only a few of the primary or secondary feathers are shed at a time.

Except for barn owls, molting of wing feathers is from the inside out. With barn owls, wing feathers are replaced from the middle of the wing out, moving in both directions. Tail feathers in most species drop out a few at a time except for some small owls, which lose all of their tail feathers at once. Whatever the pattern of molt in these important feathers, owls are never incapacitated during the process.

THE OWL DIET

"With the falling shades of night, near the abodes of mankind as well as in the remote wilderness, everywhere a countless multitude of small beasts come forth and form a little, bright-eyed furry world."
— Edward W. Nelson (*Wild Animals of North America*, 1918)

Like most birds, owls can't chew their food and the task of digestion is left entirely to their internal organs. Once swallowed, the digestive system has the task of extracting nutrition from whatever they swallow but they have relatively weak digestive juices with which to perform this task. In fact, the relative efficiency of their digestive systems has been measured at between 75 and 80 percent, meaning much of what they eat is wasted.

Owls, with few exceptions, are active year-round and eat every day. They do have some fat reserves, a traditional source of stored energy for animals, but compared to most other birds and animals, the percentage compared to their overall body weight is low. Barn owls have the least amount of fat, about 6 percent of their total body weight. Short eared owls have 9 percent; long eared owls up to 12 percent; and snowy owls even more, at least during winter months.

Food for owls is often a whole animal and little care is taken to separate edible from inedible parts in most of their meals, except for larger prey animals that can't be swallowed whole. But most of the time, owls favor food sources that can be easily swallowed. Large owl species such as the great horned owl, however, will commonly attack prey animals that are near their size or larger, depending on the shock of the attack to overcome any resistance. Even the smallest owls may occasionally make an exception and attack large prey. Pygmy owls, for instance, have been observed successfully preying on birds such as quail that weigh twice as much as they do. If unable

THE OWL MENU

ants
armadillos
bats
bees
beetles
birds
butterflies
caterpillars
centipedes
chipmunks
cicadas
crayfish
crickets
cutworms
deer mice
earthworms
fish
flies
flying squirrels
frogs
grasshoppers
grasshopper mice
ground squirrels
hares
harvest mice
kangaroo rats
lemmings
lizards
meadow voles
millipedes
moles

moths
muskrats
nutria
opossums
pikas
pocket gophers
pocket mice
porcupines
prairie dogs
rabbits
raccoons
rats
rice rats
roaches
salamanders
scorpions
shrews
skunks
snakes
spiders
toads
tree squirrels
turtles
voles
walking sticks
water bugs
water rats
weasels
white-footed mice
woodchucks
woodrats

THE RODENT MENU

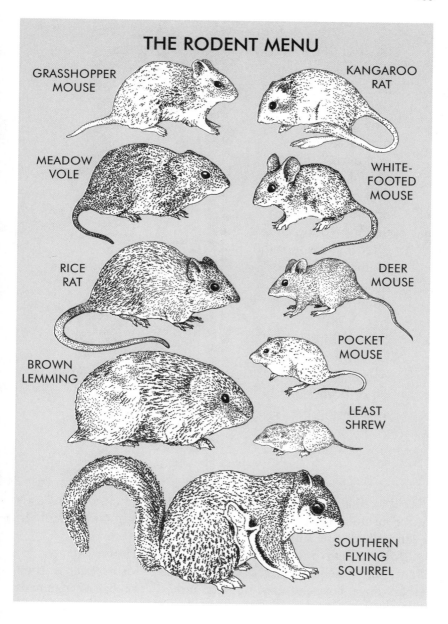

GRASSHOPPER MOUSE

KANGAROO RAT

MEADOW VOLE

WHITE-FOOTED MOUSE

RICE RAT

DEER MOUSE

POCKET MOUSE

BROWN LEMMING

LEAST SHREW

SOUTHERN FLYING SQUIRREL

Most of the time, owls eat smaller animals by swallowing them whole. Usually they grasp the animal head first in their bill, then gulp it down, tail and all. With larger animals, or when feeding young owlets, they often pull or tear the animal into two or more pieces, depending on the size. With some animals, they may discard the head, wings, or other body parts before swallowing the rest.

to kill or disable such a larger prey during an attack, the tiny owls will continue to grip their prey while they tear at it with their bills, eventually dispatching it.

Owls will also prey upon other predators. House cats, for instance, are a frequent target of great horned owls in much of their urban range. Foxes, skunks, weasels, and other predatory mammals may become a meal for a large owl if they are unfortunate enough to be in the open when the owl is searching for food. Large owls may also occasionally snatch a smaller owl for a meal.

In the nest, some owl chicks may cannibalize their siblings. This is particularly likely for broods with a wide gap in ages between the oldest and youngest chicks and during times when other food sources are scarce. With barn owls, such behavior has also been observed when the younger chicks become less active, a natural consequence of disease or malnutrition. Most of the time, older chicks display the opposite behavior, allowing younger chicks to crowd against them for warmth when the parents are away from the

Although the majority of their diet consists of rodents, owls will take advantage of the opportunity to attack and eat just about anything. This horned owl has captured a snake.

nest and in some cases, even responding to begging behavior by feeding their younger siblings.

Food sources for most owls vary throughout the year, part of the natural cycle of the animal world. Although some owls are more picky than others, most are opportunists, eating the food that is available. And because most owls spend all four seasons in the same general area, the amount of food available to them often changes with the seasons. Eastern screech owls have been found to consume more food at certain times of the year and have differing body weights in different seasons. In the winter, for example, when they burn more energy to stay warm, they eat more every day, as much as double the amount they might eat during the warmer summer months.

Although owls can be opportunistic feeders, most North American species target rodents for the majority of their diet. The barn owl has a decided preference for these small mammals, even when other prey is available. Studies of barn owl diets in North America show that in some areas, 100 percent of the food they eat comes from these small mammals. Even in areas where their diet might be more varied, no less than 70 percent of their food comes from rodents.

Owls in general have high rates of metabolism, common in most types of birds. With a metabolism that burns energy rapidly, owls are forced to hunt and eat frequently in order to survive, but there are differences in how much food different species of owls typically consume. The smallest owls have the greatest appetites. Pygmy owls, for example, often consume up to half of their body weight every day. Great horned owls, at the other extreme, may average only fifteen percent of their weight in food intake, but they can weigh up to ten times more than a pygmy owl. A burrowing owl at most would only eat 4 ounces (120 grams) in order to equal half of its own weight; a great horned owl would have to consume more than twice that much, about 10 ounces (284 grams), to equal just fifteen percent of its average weight. Barn owls consume about 5 ounces (150 grams) a day on average.

An exception to other owls are the eating habits of snowy owls. During the height of winter, birds of this species may fast for up to forty days. This is not likely by choice, but because few prey animals are available. In order to survive in such conditions, snowy owls have much higher levels of fat deposits than other owls and can respond to low food conditions by reducing their activities to a minimum, creating an almost torpid state that conserves energy.

Small owls generally spend more time hunting for food and eating it compared to the large owls. This is because their prey is typically smaller and it takes more to provide an adequate diet.

Owls eat their prey when it is dead. Their feeding method is simple and direct. With small animals they just swallow the whole body, almost always head first; with animals too large to be swallowed whole, they use their bill and talons to tear off pieces that are more bite-sized. With some prey, they may also remove and discard heads, feet, and other appendages. With captured birds, owls will generally rip the heads off of the body along with most of the bigger flight feathers before consuming the carcass. For larger mammals such as rabbits and squirrels, a piece at a time is the general rule; with their tremendous bill and talon strength, they are able to dismember even the largest prey, one limb at a time.

Some owls, particularly great horned owls and snowy owls, may react to excesses in local food availability by eating food more selectively. In one observed case, for example, owls continuously raided a large colony of rats and choose to eat only the brains of these rodents, leaving behind the rest of the head and bodies.

Owls that frequently prey upon birds may use "feather perches" when hunting. These platforms, usually close to the nest, are a convenient stopping point where the owls take the birds after capture. Using their bills and talons, the major flight feathers are stripped off the carcass at this site, leaving a more comfortable meal to swallow.

HUNTING FOR FOOD

"When one considers the character of this Owl's song in connection with his bill of fare, it is not surprising that the former is somewhat indicative of the nature of the latter. What with mice, small birds, snakes, and frogs as a standard diet, why should not one's song savor of the terrible, and cause the listener's blood to run cold!"

— F. Schuyler Matthews
(Fieldbook of Wild Birds and Their Music, 1904)

Owls are formidable predators. Like all raptors, they are efficient at locating and catching their prey, but they possess keener eyesight and hearing than their competitors. And unlike other raptors, they dive on their prey without the telltale sound of air rushing through feathers. Being silent predators, the small animals that are their prey cannot hear them coming.

Though they possess keen eyesight, owls are not equipped to see in total darkness. But even on moonless nights, starlight provides enough illumination for owls to find prey, given their remarkable vision. Their acute sense of hearing also adds a powerful backup, as well as a "first alert" system, capable of detecting prey by sound before it is in sight. Not only are owls capable of hearing the faintest noises from a distance, the placement of their ears gives them an efficient distance-and-location measuring system.

Some studies with captive owls indicate that there are also other factors that aid in the hunting success. Owls that stay in the same, familiar locations for their hunting activities learn and remember where they are most likely to find prey. Prime feeding locations for rodents or open areas where small animals travel without cover are targeted for repeated hunting missions. And as owls fly through these same zones, they learn and remember the location of trees, branches, and other obstacles. Such familiarity can improve hunting success because it allows owls to focus more on their prey and less on their flying routes.

Among the North American species, most hunting is done by perching and waiting for prey to appear. The larger owls, however, may sometimes hunt "on the wing," that is by searching for prey while soaring. When perching, owls often develop favorite ambush sites, using the same vantage points over and over.

Most birds of prey dive on their targets, using speed to achieve surprise. Owls can dive, but may also "flap" their way to a target, taking a more leisurely pace because, unlike other raptors, they are less likely to be heard by their target on the way in. Studies of barn owls using infrared cameras, for example, indicate they may beat their wings throughout an attack on their prey, including at the moment of contact. But this hunting method is most likely when the owl is flying in very dark conditions. Studies of owl strikes in daylight or dim lighting show that they are more likely to glide toward the prey and not flap their wings. The same barn owls that flapped all the way to the target, for instance, chose to glide when there was more light.

In many cases, owls hunt from low branches, stumps, or fence posts, putting them only a short distance from their target. Rather than flap, glide, or dive, owls may simply drop off their perches and jump onto their targets, opening their wings only at the last minute. Surrounded by potentially harmful snags and obstacles, this technique helps reduce the possibility of snagging wings and feathers on the way down.

In owl strikes that come from the air, the incoming owl keeps its head in line with the target almost all the way, pulling the head back only at the last minute while simultaneously thrusting its feet forward — which in normal flight are kept close to the body and pointed back — and opening the talons wide, two pointed forward and two to the rear. One study of barn owl hunting showed that they closed their eyes just as their talons were striking their prey.

During a
diving attack
on their prey, owls
maintain a steady visual
lock on their target until just
before they reach it.
Only a second or two before the
strike, they use their wings and tails to suddenly slow
their flight, thrust their feet forward and pull their
heads back. The strike is made with one or both feet
and talons, and the force of impact is enough to stun
most small animals.

Owls strike with their talons. Heavy bones in their legs and feet are well designed to withstand the impact of hitting a prey animal while in full flight. The impact of the strike as well as the pincer-like grasp of the talons usually renders the prey helpless. Stunned and immobilized at the same stroke, prey animals are then immediately killed with a snap of the owl's powerful bill. Owls that have made a kill on the ground often spread their wings and tail, "covering" the prey as if protecting it from other predators. Within a few seconds, the owl flies off, carrying the prey in one foot; on occasion, they may carry prey in their bills.

Flammulated owls are an exception to this hunting technique. Feeding almost entirely on insects — most often flying insects — they usually catch most of their prey in the air by snatching it with their bills. Other owls may also occasionally track and attack birds while they are in the air, but they typically use their talons at the moment of impact.

During winter months, some owls also hunt by locating prey under blankets of snow. Great gray owls, boreal owls, and hawk owls have been seen plunging from the air into snow-covered fields in quest of small rodents. The rodents are located by sound; owls capture them by diving into the cover over their estimated locations. If they miss on the first leap, they may make successive bounds through the snow to locate their quarry.

Great horned owls are also proficient at flushing tree squirrels out of protective foliage or nests, spooking them into the open where they can be snagged. Tree squirrels are most vulnerable early in the day and early in the evening, the beginning and end of their activity cycles and the reverse for most owls. Great horned owls have been observed hunting for tree squirrels in daylight hours by slamming into the squirrels' nests. The collision forces any squirrels inside to scurry for safety, leaving them in the open and vulnerable.

Most of the squirrels that become meals for owls, however, are flying squirrels, active in the night like the owls. In some parts of their range, owls are the major predator for these tiny soaring rodents.

Owls develop hunting patterns when they have regular hunting territory. The discovery of a regular source of food may keep them coming back, often at the same time of day or night. This has been noted with several species, especially great horned owls, which have been observed making repeated raids on birds which traditionally nest in colonies, including ducks and crows.

Variations in owl hunting techniques are also used when prey other than rodents is on the menu. Owls are very successful at snagging smaller birds out of the air. They may also attempt to flush prey from dense thickets or trees. Some owls can also fish. In this case, unlike with other raptors which dive onto a swimming target, an owl may wade in shallow water and strike at anything that moves, including crayfish, water snakes, and frogs. When fishing, these owls can also skim over the surface of a stream or lake, snatching fish on the fly, or perching quietly at the edge of the

Most owls carry their prey in one or both feet after making a kill. Smaller species such as the burrowing owl sometimes carry their favorite food — insects — in their bills.

water, grabbing any fish that surfaces near them. John James Audubon, in *The Birds of America*, wrote about one such fishing expedition he witnessed on the Ohio River near Louisville, Kentucky. There, a large snowy owl was seen hiding on a rock, waiting for fish to surface near it, then "it thrust out the foot next the water, and, with the quickness of lightning, seized it, and drew it out."

Small owls that feed primarily on insects often spend time flushing them out of branches, brush, or ground cover. Owls may also walk or hop along the ground, seeking earthworms, other insects, or small mammals that they may come across. Some naturalists also believe that owls may occasionally dig their prey out of protected holes in the ground, using their talons to uncover the prey.

When sufficient prey is available, barn owls have been known to follow a methodical hunting schedule. The first hunt is early in the evening, sometimes before the sun sets. A second hunt comes around midnight; a third at the end of the night or as the sun rises. Other night-hunting owls may also hunt just before dark or just after daybreak, taking advantage of prey activity that often peaks during these periods.

Hunting patterns are affected by the type of prey owls catch. With larger prey, owls may hunt less often each night because each animal they catch provides more food. An owl may also alter its hunting pattern if it is itself threatened, such as when a great horned owl is on the wing in the territory of a smaller owl. And if a mated pair of owls is feeding a brood, additional flights may be required.

A very small owl like the flammulated owl feeds almost entirely on insects and arachnids. Whether feeding just themselves or a brood, these owls are often much more active than larger owls, hunting throughout a nighttime period. When feeding their young, small owls also typically only catch one prey animal at a time before returning to the nest, requiring many flights each night. In one study, flammulated owls that had young chicks in the nest made almost ten trips an hour between their hunting grounds and their nest. During the incubation period, they made less than half this number of trips.

Elf owls have been observed making almost one trip to the nest every minute during a peak feeding frenzy, a captured insect delivered with each trip. The great gray owl, the largest owl species in North America, also hunts with greater frequency during some periods of the year. This owl, unlike the other large owls, prefers smaller prey such as voles and pocket gophers, with half or more of its diet consisting of these tiny mammals. In order to provide enough food for itself, more hunting trips are necessary.

Owls are efficient, opportunistic hunters. While there may be a food source that is favored, most often this is due to that food source being the most abundant in their hunting territory. With insects, it is only the warmer months of the year.

Almost always, owls consume what they eat soon after it has been caught. Some species, however, store food in caches for later consumption. Northern pygmy owls, barn owls, and short eared owls stash dead prey animals when there are chicks in the nest; this behavior has also been observed with great horned owls. The short eared owl's strategy may help reduce aggression among chicks because the supply of food close at hand encourages them to feed on it rather than each other. Some large owls may also feed on carrion at some times, including animals that are not part of their regular diet.

Domestic animals are usually safe from attack by owls. Typically, most of these animals are inside enclosures during nighttime hours and few are small enough to be handled by even the largest owls. Exceptions include house cats, small dogs, chickens, and other small fowl. Domestic fowl as large as turkeys, however, have been killed by great horned owls. And when flocks of ducks or chickens are kept in open pens, great horned owls have sometimes become

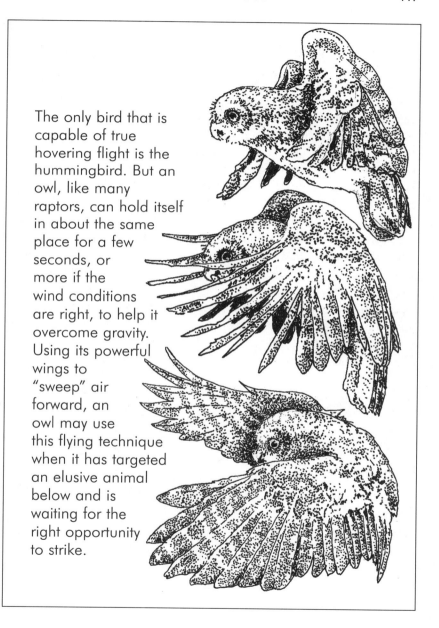

The only bird that is capable of true hovering flight is the hummingbird. But an owl, like many raptors, can hold itself in about the same place for a few seconds, or more if the wind conditions are right, to help it overcome gravity. Using its powerful wings to "sweep" air forward, an owl may use this flying technique when it has targeted an elusive animal below and is waiting for the right opportunity to strike.

major pests, returning frequently to these sites for their easy pick-ing. In some cases, owls may even enter a poorly secured roosting area and snatch resting hens off their perches.

Most species of North American owls reside year-round in their home range. Breeding seasons for all species are loosely coordi-nated with the larger cycle of life in their local ecosystems. When most chicks are hatched, it is usually early in the spring, often before migratory birds have made their annual appearance. As the chicks near the end of their brooding period and prepare to add their hunting activities to those of their parents, the time has usu-ally arrived for the full force of natural reproduction, bringing migratory birds, new generations of wintering birds, and new gen-erations of local prey animals, from rodents to insects. Thus, just as they are learning to hunt on their own, there is an abundance of food to hunt for, increasing the young owls chance of survival.

Larger owls such as the great horned owl are also known to prey upon smaller owls. In one published report from early in this cen-tury, a barred owl was examined after being shot and found to have a partially digested long eared owl in its stomach; in the stomach of the long eared owl was found the body of an eastern screech owl.

OWL PELLETS

"Ill-omen'd in his form, the unlucky fowl,
Abhorr'd by men, and call'd a scrieching owl."
— Ovid (*The Metamorphoses,* 8 A.D.)

Unlike other birds, owls have no crops. This part of the avian anatomy, a loose sac located in the throat, provides a handy storage container for holding food for later consumption, but owls, being without, funnel all of their food directly into their digestive systems. All the smaller animals they eat, being consumed whole, are digested in the gizzard where digestive fluids dissolve all the usable tissue except for fur and bones. But this digestive fluid, in combination with the large chunks of material it has to work with, only dissolves soft tissue such as muscle, skin, and fat.

What is left behind is the bones, often unbroken, and everything that couldn't be extracted by the gizzard, including feathers, fur, teeth, skulls, and claws. This mass, too large and dangerous to pass through the rest of the owl's digestive tract, is regurgitated as a compact pellet. Owl pellets have long been used to provide researchers with accurate information about the species of prey consumed, because the pellets typically include a complete skull, the most useful body feature in identifying small mammals.

Owl pellets vary in size depending on the species of owl. The general rule is, the larger the species, the larger the pellet, although the largest owls do not have pellets much different in size than medium-sized owls. Owl pellets may vary in size due to the size of the prey animal, the time of year, and the length of digestive time inside the owl. And if startled or otherwise interrupted, an owl might prematurely engorge a pellet that is larger than it would be if retained for a longer period in its digestive system.

A pellet reaches its final form a few hours after the owl eats but it is not immediately ejected. Instead, it travels up from the gizzard

OWL PELLET GUIDE

SPECIES	PELLET DESCRIPTION
BARN OWL	large size, smooth, cylindrical, rounded both ends, dark color
BARRED OWL	large size, solidly compacted
BOREAL OWL	about 1½", dark gray color
BURROWING OWL	about 1", smooth, brown color
EASTERN SCREECH OWL	1"–1½", oval, solidly compacted, dark gray color
ELF OWL	very small size, dry and loosely compacted
FERRUGINOUS PYGMY OWL	small size, oval shape, solidly compacted
FLAMMULATED OWL	small size, loosely compacted
GREAT GRAY OWL	very large size
GREAT HORNED OWL	3"–4" long, cylindrical, solidly compacted, light to dark gray color
LONG-EARED OWL	1½"–2", irregular in shape, gray color
NORTHERN HAWK OWL	small size, gray color
NORTHERN PYGMY OWL	very small size, very loosely compacted, pellets rarely formed
NORTHERN SAW-WHET OWL	½"–¾", solidly compacted, dark gray color
SHORT-EARED OWL	about 2", rounded one end, tapered one end, gray to dark gray color
SNOWY OWL	very large size, loosely compacted, irregular in shape
SPOTTED OWL	large size, solidly compacted
WESTERN SCREECH OWL	1"–1½", oval, solidly compacted, dark gray color
WHISKERED SCREECH OWL	small size, loosely compacted

OWL PELLETS

SNOWY OWL

HORNED OWL

SCREECH OWL

BARN OWL

SHORT-EARED OWL

SAW-WHET OWL

LONG-EARED OWL

into an enlarged space just above the gizzard, a unique part of bird anatomy called the proventriculus. This anatomical structure is connected to the gullet, or esophagus, and can be used to store a pellet for as long as eight or ten hours. Because the position of the finished pellet partially blocks the digestive system, an owl cannot swallow new food until it has regurgitated the remains of the last meal. The regurgitation of a pellet is often the signal that an owl is ready to eat again. When an owl eats more than one animal within a few hours, their remains are consolidated into one pellet.

The pellet cycle is a regular one for owls. Following a consistent schedule, they regurgitate these masses when their digestive systems have finished extracting nutrition. For barn owls, pellets are ejected eight to twelve hours after the food has first entered their systems. One pellet is normally ejected at the beginning of their "day," which is actually early evening, just before they begin hunting. Another is ejected at the end of the night, when they have returned to the nesting site to begin a resting cycle. Some owls eject pellets up to twenty hours after food has been ingested.

The process of regurgitation may take from a few seconds up to a few minutes. Contractions of the esophagus force the pellet upward in spasms that may make an owl resemble a human coughing or retching. Although the ejection may look uncomfortable, it doesn't hurt the owl because the pellet covering protects it from the sharp bits of bone contained within. Also, the exterior is covered with a coating of slimy digestive liquid, that acts as a lubricant.

Pellet shapes and textures vary according to the species of the owl and the type of prey animal. At one extreme, a single pellet might include only bits of bones and fur; at the other extreme, one pellet might have an entire bird wing. Moist when first ejected, pellets rapidly dry out and will usually begin decomposing quickly.

Many owl chicks are fed only bits of animals or insects for the first week or so after they hatch. Until they begin swallowing their first whole animals, they don't produce pellets.

Other birds that disgorge pellets include hawks, eagles, gulls, swallows, dippers, and swifts, although the pellets from these species are almost always smaller and contain fewer animal parts than those from owls. Owl pellets may also be mistaken for the droppings of some mammals, especially foxes. The differences: fox droppings are almost always in open areas, away from trees and are found as a single unit; a musty smell is also present. Owl pellets are typically found in piles under branches where owls regularly perch, and usually have little odor unless they begin decomposing.

Owls not only regurgitate pellets, they generate more traditional kinds of bird wastes. Liquid feces and urine are deposited on a regular basis and owl perches are stained with the remnants of this waste, a liquid called whitewash. Like the name suggests, this is usually white, but it may also be a darker color or be streaked with other colors, including brown, gray, green, or black.

PELLET CONTENTS

A single owl pellet contains all the undigestible parts of an owl's latest meal, including whole and broken bones. The contents illustrated here came from a great horned owl with a hunting territory on the open plains near Denver, Colorado. The animal: plains pocket gopher. Shown actual size.

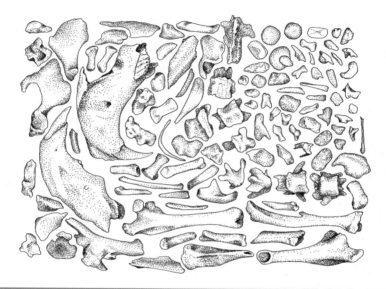

WARNING

Owl pellets contain organic materials that can transmit harmful bacteria such as salmonella. Dangerous viruses such as the hantavirus may also be contracted through such items. Any owl pellet should be handled only while wearing protective gloves and a dust mask. To be safe, the pellets should first be heated in a conventional oven while wrapped in aluminum foil. Bake the pellets for 45–60 minutes at 300° F. The heat kills bacteria and viruses but will not harm the tiny bones and other contents of the pellets.

REPRODUCTION

"Solemnity is what they express — fit representatives of the night." — Henry David Thoreau (December 14, 1858, *Journal*)

Most owls reach sexual maturity and are ready to reproduce about a year after they are born. Some of the larger species, however, may not begin breeding until their second or third year. Variations in when reproduction begins may also be connected to local or annual variations in the availability of food. When prey is bountiful, some owl species are known to take advantage by beginning their reproductive life early. But even when able and ready to reproduce, not all owls may reproduce every year. Variations in the breeding schedule may correspond to the weather, the availability of food locally, competition from other owls, availability of acceptable mating partners, and disease.

Owls begin their annual mating season earlier than most birds. With few exceptions, owl species in North America are permanent residents, and are already established in the territory where they hunt and nest, giving them a head start in the reproduction cycle. Some owls begin mating rituals as early as January, others might not begin until February or March. And for some species, mating may begin at different times depending on where the owls are in their geographical range. In general, mating begins earlier to the south and later to the north. Snowy owls occupy the most northerly range of all North American species and, always affected by the colder climate, begin breeding later than other owls, sometimes as late as May.

Barn owls usually begin their mating rituals in late winter. The male birds use a special call during the mating season to attract females to their territory. As the male courts a female, much of their activity is on the wing, with one bird chasing the other through the air while both utter loud calls. Males may also perform a unique "moth flight" during courtship. This stunt involves hovering in front of a perched female, almost as if the male is "flashing" her with the distinctive white areas on its chest and belly. A male may also attempt to divert female interest to his nest site by repeatedly flying back and forth from this platform. When a female finally takes notice of the male and begins to respond, it is with another unique mating call, this one a series of snorting sounds that are similar to the calls that owl chicks make when they are begging for food. And in response, the interested male will often present the female with a freshly caught animal. This offering frequently seals the deal for the male; copulation often occurs after the female feeds. In most other owl species, the males also use offerings of food as part of the mating ritual, although females may respond even without such presents. When females do become receptive to males, there is often a period of mutual preening, with both owls perched close together. At some point in this process — which may last only a few minutes or extend to an hour or more — the male and the female may use other special mating calls, which include coos, whistles, soft hooting, or bill clicking. During the process of copulation, an act that rarely lasts more than a few seconds, other calls may be emitted, including unique copulation screams from either the male or the female, or both. Preening sessions and copulation may be repeated up to several times, but the mating cycle usually lasts for only a day or two. With some owls, it may extend for a few days longer.

The adult owls usually begin a nesting phase at about the same time that they are mating. Nesting can begin days before mating or begin right after mating. Owls are notoriously lax in their nest-building activity and this nesting phase primarily consists of finding and occupying suitable sites. For owl species in North America, this mostly consists of locating and taking over a suitable nest or nesting site from some other animal. For tree-nesting owls, these are nests usually built by other large birds or tree squirrels. Sometimes, using the same nest year after year, no additional nesting rituals are required after the owl pair has copulated. Even before there are eggs to brood, female owls may begin acting as if they are brooding, spending most of their time in the nest.

A single copulation can provide enough semen from the male to fertilize all of the eggs a female will lay, but multiple copulations can also provide a continuing supply. Copulation usually leads to fertilization within a day or two and can happen within a few hours. As each egg cell is fertilized, it passes through several different parts of the female reproductive system. The developing egg, the yolk, picks up multiple coatings of albumen (egg white) in one stage, then gets two coatings of material that will quickly develop into a shell and a shell lining. After copulation, the first egg may be ready for laying in as little as twenty-four hours. As soon as the egg shell has been deposited on the albumen, the egg is ready to enter the world and another egg is at the beginning of the same process, on a more-or-less regular cycle. The first eggs are laid one every twenty-four to forty-eight hours, depending on the species of owls. After a few eggs are laid, the cycle may become more erratic, with several days between subsequent eggs. As soon as the eggs appear, incubation can begin.

During incubation, owls rarely leave the nest, typically only a few times a day in order to defecate and get water. Ground-nesting species have the greatest challenge during incubation because the typical lack of nesting material places more responsibility on the nesting parent to provide ample warmth to the developing eggs. Female owls, like most female birds, meet this challenge with a unique adaptation to their plumage, a sparsely feathered area on their bellies called a brood patch. This almost naked skin has a higher percentage of blood vessels than other parts of the skin, providing a direct source of heat from the mother's body to the eggs. Snowy owls lay their eggs directly onto bare frozen ground and have developed very large brood patches to compensate for the climate.

OWL EGGS

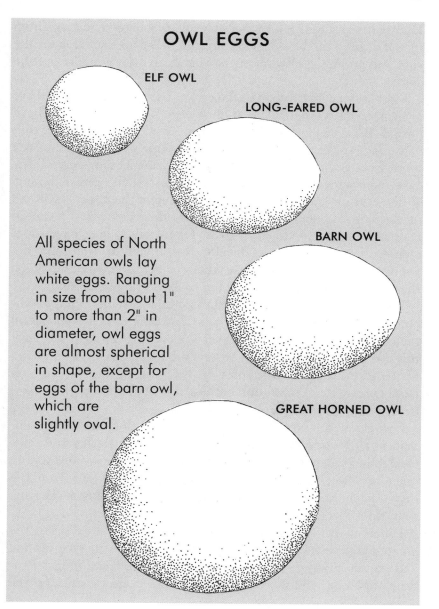

ELF OWL

LONG-EARED OWL

BARN OWL

GREAT HORNED OWL

All species of North American owls lay white eggs. Ranging in size from about 1" to more than 2" in diameter, owl eggs are almost spherical in shape, except for eggs of the barn owl, which are slightly oval.

During the brooding phase, owls may pluck their own feathers from in and around the brood patch, creating more contact area for the eggs and providing loose feathers which can also help insulate the eggs.

Most owls begin incubating the eggs as soon as the first is laid but some may not begin incubation until a few hours or a few days have passed. Because eggs are laid at a rate of about one every two to three days, the earliest eggs may be up to three weeks older than the latest in large broods. A few species delay incubation until all the eggs have appeared, a strategy that helps synchronize hatching. When eggs are incubated from the beginning, the result is a brood of chicks with greatly differing stages of development, a common feature for owl broods. Barn owls, for instance, may have older chicks that have already developed feathers by the time the youngest chicks hatch, allowing them to help their mother brood the youngest chicks and freeing her to leave the nest to hunt.

The first two or three eggs laid sometimes exhibit a unique synchronization, with these early chicks hatching in a shorter period than the time span that separated their laying. Biologists believe this may be a natural strategy to give the first chicks a headstart in nourishment and more support by the parents; later chicks are more vulnerable to starvation because it is harder to find food for a larger number of chicks.

Owl chicks are born with an "egg tooth," a unique feature common to all birds. Developed while inside the egg, this protrusion is used to help them chip their way out of the tough eggshell. Within one to two weeks after hatching the egg tooth drops out. From the first moment of hatching they also have the ability to make begging sounds for food.

Different owl species have different food begging calls, but the greatest difference among the species is between the tree-nesting and ground-nesting species. Above ground level, owl chicks typically are louder and more aggressive in their begging calls; on the ground, chicks are typically quieter and less noticeable, a development that helps keep them out of the hearing of predators. Owl chicks rapidly become very active and well-developed. Born blind and with a thin coating of down, in only one to two weeks a second coat of heavier down appears, giving them more protection. Young owls in species with ear tufts are not born with these distinctive features. Only after their down begins to be replaced with adult plumage do these upright feathers emerge.

From the first day, owlets rapidly develop strength and alertness. Some chicks are actually able to clamber out of their nests before they are three weeks old, well before their first flight feathers appear. Among ground-nesting owls, the young chicks may wander far away from the nest, staying hidden in vegetation or crevices in rocky terrain. Barn owl chicks also exhibit this precocious behavior, wandering out of their nesting spots when they are only four weeks old.

Young barn owls fledge, or take their first flights, at the age of 56 to 62 days. Within a few days of their first flights, these juvenile owls may begin drifting away from home. At the same point in time, their parents may cease to feed them, actively chase them away from the nest, or abandon the nest entirely during their own daily roosting periods, forcing the young owls to quickly fend for themselves.

Some owl species seem to be monogamous, mating for life. Screech owls are one such example, but they will quickly adopt new mates if one dies. Other owl species may bond for only a single breeding season or even a single brood. Sometimes, different mates may be selected when multiple broods are reared in a single year.

As the chicks hatch, the parents immediately begin to provide food for them. For most species, whole animals are fed from the very beginning, although the animals are mostly small rodents or insects, a size able to be swallowed whole even by the youngest chicks. Spotted owls, on the other hand, often tear the heads off

Great horned owl four weeks after hatching.

Great horned owl nine days after hatching.

the rodents and birds that are captured for the chicks; the parents feed the chicks bits of the prey ripped off with their bills rather than the whole animal. Great horned owls coordinate their hunting targets with the size of the chicks. When they are newly hatched and small in size, the food selected for them is also small. As they grow, the menu expands to include ever larger meals.

Within a few weeks, most owl chicks are strong enough to handle their own food when it is brought to the nest, pulling feathers off of birds and ripping heads off of small mammals before they are swallowed. Young owls also begin producing pellets as soon as they begin eating whole animals, or animal parts that contain fur, bones, and other indigestible pieces.

A few owl species in North America may reproduce more than once a year. Such multiple broods are often a response to a local abundance of food, but even if a single brood is the normal practice, many owl species will sometimes produce a second brood in response to a catastrophe befalling their first brood. If it is early enough in the season and the eggs or chicks are destroyed by disease, malnutrition, or predators, the parents may respond by breeding again. This could also be the case when windstorms or lightning destroy a nest.

The barn owl is the only species in North America that will regularly produce more than one brood a year. In some cases, the broods overlap, with eggs in the second clutch being laid while juvenile birds from the first brood are still in the nest and being fed by the parents.

OWL NESTS

"The gravest bird's an owl."

— Allan Ramsay
(*Scots Proverbs*, 1737)

Except for the barn owl, which has become uniquely identified with nests in man-made structures, owls usually find appropriate homesites in wild terrain. Natural cavities in tree trunks are a favorite of many owls, holes that have been created by decay, dropped limbs, fire, lightning, or woodpeckers. Some also seek out and use large nests built by other birds such as eagles, hawks, or crows. It is also not uncommon for an owl to usurp a nest constructed by a tree squirrel or use one that has been abandoned. Ledges, niches, and overhangs on cliffs or in caves are also acceptable locations for most above-ground owl nesters.

When suitable nesting sites are available and other conditions remain stable, some owl species continually favor the same nesting sites from year to year. In some cases, this habit may last for many years; at the extreme, there are records of nesting sites used for up to fifty years.

In most cases, owls do not go to elaborate lengths to make a nesting site comfortable or secure. Barn owls, for example, usually create a nest simply by selecting a perching area, with no nesting material gathered or arranged. Any padding or protection for the eggs and chicks comes only from the regurgitated pellets that barn owls typically leave in the nest area. In many owl nests, the only secondary material present is discarded owl feathers and bits and pieces of fur and feathers from prey animals. In tree cavities, wood chips and natural debris from the tree may also form a minimal cushion.

Although owls may keep their feathers clean, their nest sites are another matter. Constructed of rudimentary materials and rarely including any lining, owl nests are a mess. In addition, eggs — white

NESTING SITES

BARN OWL	cavities in trees or cliffs; ledges in barns, abandoned buildings, or towers
BARRED OWL	cavities in trees, or in abandoned crow, hawk, or squirrel nests, occasionally nests on ground or low shrubs
BOREAL OWL	cavities in trees, prefers conifers
BURROWING OWL	excavated burrows, burrows made by prairie dogs, skunks, foxes, badgers, or armadillos
EASTERN SCREECH OWL	cavities in trees
ELF OWL	cavities in saguaro cactus and trees
FERRUGINOUS PYGMY OWL	cavities in trees and crevices in rocky terrain
FLAMMULATED OWL	cavities in trees, prefers conifers
GREAT GRAY OWL	abandoned hawk nests high in trees, prefers conifers
GREAT HORNED OWL	abandoned hawk, eagle, or crow nests in hardwood trees or conifers, also may use cavities in cliffs; occasionally nests on ground
LONG-EARED OWL	abandoned crow, hawk, or squirrel nests; occasionally nests on ground
NORTHERN HAWK OWL	cavities in trees or abandoned nests
NORTHERN PYGMY OWL	cavities in trees
NORTHERN SAW-WHET OWL	cavities in trees
SHORT-EARED OWL	nests on ground in concealed vegetation; occasionally uses burrow
SNOWY OWL	nests on ground, rocky surfaces, or cliffs
SPOTTED OWL	cavities in trees or abandoned hawk or raven nests, prefers conifers
WESTERN SCREECH OWL	cavities in trees
WHISKERED SCREECH OWL	cavities in trees

or near-white upon laying — often become splotched and discolored by the time chicks hatch, coated with excrement and bits of uneaten prey animals.

Some owls, including great horned owls, great gray owls, and spotted owls, do add some insulation to their nests in order to protect the eggs and chicks. This most often consists of feathers and down plucked from their own bodies but may include evergreen sprigs, moss, and bark chips. Burrowing owls are another exception. These birds frequently add grass, plant stalks, and dried manure chips to their nesting holes. Like the burrowing owls, short-eared owls are also ground nesters and typically take advantage of local materials to line their nests. This material may include grass, plant stalks, and other vegetation.

Owls that construct their own nests may first find a site that takes the least preparation. Tree trunks or stumps with hollows where branches have fallen present one option, but just about any level surface that is high enough off the ground may be selected. When owls choose to use the ground, they may also either take

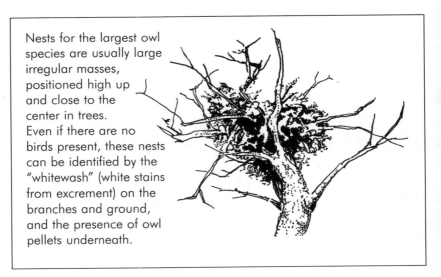

Nests for the largest owl species are usually large irregular masses, positioned high up and close to the center in trees. Even if there are no birds present, these nests can be identified by the "whitewash" (white stains from excrement) on the branches and ground, and the presence of owl pellets underneath.

over a suitable hollow or tunnel already created by another animal or dig their own. Barn owls in some western regions, for example, frequently select shallow cliffs and dirt banks for their nest sites. Where the soil has the appropriate texture and density, they will excavate a ledge or short tunnel with their feet. Burrowing owls, which almost always live in tunnels underground (from five to ten feet in length) frequently select their sites simply by moving into tunnels already dug by other animals such as prairie dogs, wood-chucks, ground squirrels, and foxes. But they can and do dig their own burrows when necessary, a practice most often found where soft, sandy soil makes for easy digging. To excavate a burrow, they use their bills and feet.

Among the larger owls, the practice of using nests built by other birds is widespread. Often, because owls are permanent residents of an area, they may find such a nest that has been naturally aban-doned by another bird, a species that follows a migratory cycle and is not in the nesting area for part of the year. But owls have also been observed "stealing" nests from other birds, even when the nest is recently constructed or actively occupied. Evidence such as bro-ken eggshells has also indicated that owls may sometimes destroy the former nest tenants rather than just chase them away.

When taking over squirrel nests, great horned owls and other large species may simply squash the squirrels' constructions — usu-ally a hollow tangle of twigs, small branches, and leaves — to cre-ate an open platform. In some parts of the country, owls may share a nest with other birds and squirrels, although the nesting activity is not at the same time for the different animals. The squirrels and other birds take advantage of the empty structure before or after the owls have raised their broods.

MORTALITY AND DISEASE

"On the coming on of a storm, they respond to each other in such unearthly and strange tones, that one can not help thinking that something extraordinary is taking place among them."

— Jacob H. Studer
(*The Birds of North America*, 1895)

Once they reach adult size, owls are close to or at the top of the food chain and are threatened by few other animals. Larger raptors may attack owls if given the opportunity, but usually prefer to select more suitable targets. Large owl species may even attack smaller owl species, but in most habitats this is not a usual practice because hunting territories and habits keep them separated. As in most of the animal kingdom, what most affects owl survival is the vulnerability of the young and encounters with human civilization.

Owls typically lay a large number of eggs, although the number can vary considerably. Perhaps due to the availability of food, the severity of the weather in the breeding season, or competition, an owl clutch can vary from one or two eggs to more than ten. The larger the number of eggs, however, the greater the risk of mortality to the chicks. With more mouths to feed, more chicks are likely to be underfed and die of malnourishment.

In some extremes, when there is a low cycle in prey populations, some owl species may not breed at all. At the other extreme, when prey is plentiful but a clutch of eggs or a brood of chicks has been killed by predators or died from some other cause, owl parents may immediately begin producing a new clutch of eggs.

Depending on the species, the success of owls in raising their young varies considerably. The larger owl species seem to be more successful. Studies of great horned owls, for example, indicate they may be more than 75 percent successful, on average, in raising chicks. Smaller owls, on the other hand, may have less than 50 percent success and the rate can even be as low as 15 percent.

Eggs that are abandoned or chicks that die can result from human interference as much as the lack of food. Particularly as human development cuts into breeding territories, owls that have started families are scared away from their nest sites, with some species more skittish than others. In a few long-term studies, the average number of owls successfully reared in a given area dropped significantly at the same time that human activity around them increased.

OWL PREDATORS

RED FOX

RED-SHOULDERED HAWK

MINK

COYOTE

RATTLESNAKE

Owl eggs and chicks also fall prey to animal predators. Snakes, reptiles, raccoons, tree squirrels, possums, foxes, crows, ravens, and gulls are some of the animals that will take advantage of an unprotected nest to grab a quick meal. Once young owls develop their first set of flight feathers and leave the nest, they are still more vulnerable than adults. The biggest threat to them is their lack of experience, leading them into danger and often keeping them less well-fed than older birds. Until they become proficient at finding and catching prey, avoiding predators, and flying well, they are much more likely to be injured or killed.

As they leave the nest, young owls may be ignored or even chased away by their parents. Pushed out of the family territory early in life and with little experience to guide them, they are forced into unfamiliar and distant hunting territory — strange terrain where they have no familiarity with suitable prey. Worse, the new territory is likely to already be populated with other owls, ready and willing to defend their turf against the young immigrants.

Bad weather, predators, disease, and encounters with manmade objects are also threats to the good health of young and mature owls. Collisions with cars are always close to the top of this list — one of the leading causes of death for most owls of any age. This unfortunate statistic comes from the beneficial hunting habitat that is inadvertently created by roads and highways, wide open spaces that make spotting prey easy. Other unfortunate encounters include collisions with broadcast towers and power poles, electrocution from power lines, and death from firearms.

In earlier eras, owls were a prime target for hunters, not just because they were considered pests that preyed upon domestic fowl, but because they were large flying targets that tempted the aim of many people with guns in their hands. For the largest owl species, especially the great horned owl, shooting is still the primary cause of death for adult owls in parts of their range.

From the time they leave the nest until they are about a year old, youthful owls suffer a mortality rate of 50–70 percent. Once they pass the first year marker and are adults, both in size and experience, threats to owls diminish. Adult owls suffer an annual mortality rate of 15–30 percent, but it varies from species to species and depends greatly on annual weather conditions and availability of food.

Although rare, owls may end up the losers when attacking some prey animals. Large snakes, porcupines, skunks, and house cats may occasionally turn the tables on the attacking owl, inflicting wounds that can attract disease and death.

HOW LONG CAN OWLS LIVE?

In the wild, most owls live for no more than 10 years, but they can live much longer. Based on data gathered from banded birds, these are the current records for owl longevity.

barn owl	15 years
barred owl	18 years
eastern screech owl	13 years
great horned owl	19 years
long-eared owl	27 years

In captivity and away from the hazards and stress of the wild, owls have lived even longer.

great gray owl	40 years
great horned owl	38 years
snowy owl	35 years

Lice are one of the major health problems for owls. Parasitic feather lice are widespread among owls and have evolved to live primarily only on this host animal. Fleas and a variety of flies may pester owls, but most are attracted more to the messy contents of an owl nest than the host.

Hepatosplentitis infectiosa strigum is a viral disease that can be fatal to owls, but a few species — including the barn owl and genus Strix owls — are naturally immune. Owls are also susceptible to tuberculosis, malarial infections, aspergillosis (a fungus that infects the lungs), pneumonia, and a variety of parasitic worms.

Owls that feed on pigeons may also catch something from their prey, a parasitic protozoa that multiplies in the esophagus and trachea, creating a cheesy deposit — referred to as *frounce* by falconers, owners of other raptors that get this disease — that can choke a bird to death. Other diseases that can be transmitted by birds that are eaten by owls include salmonella, Newcastle's disease, cholera, and botulism.

OWL CALLS

*"Spectral creatures of the night are the owls,
that flit here and there on noiseless wings."*
— William Atherton DuPuy (*Our Bird Friends and Foes*, 1925)

Owls, perhaps more than most birds, display a wide range of calls when communicating with other owls. These include not only a variety of hoots, but also screeches, purrs, wails, warning screams, mobbing notes, anxiety calls, distress calls, defensive hissing, courtship hisses, snorts, twitters, chittering, chattering, squeaking, and tongue-clicking. Many owls also occasionally use their wings to make noise, most often as part of a mating display. The wings, usually quiet in normal operation, are slapped together either above or below the owl's body, making clapping sounds that can vary in intensity.

The hooting that is most often associated with owls is often communications relating to territory. Hooting announces to other owls that a piece of property is in one owl's possession and trespassing is not welcomed. Hooting may also be used by a male owl to attract females — owls of the same species are able to recognize suitable mates. The pitch, or deepness, of an owl's hoot is also directly related to their size; in general, the bigger the owl, the deeper the hooting. One exception to this rule is the flammulated owl, which, despite its tiny size, has a deep, booming call. Despite the fact that in many owl species the females are larger than the males, the males usually have calls that are deeper in pitch. Here, too, however, there is at least one exception. Female barn owls, larger than male barn owls, also have the deeper call of the two genders.

Owls, because of their nighttime lifestyle, are often difficult to spot and identify, but their calls make up for this deficiency. Professional birdwatchers and amateur birders both use owl calls as

OWL CALLS

SPECIES	MAJOR IDENTIFYING CALL
BARN OWL	single, drawn-out "screeee"
BARRED OWL	deep-pitched resonant "hoo, hoo, hoooo, aa" with emphasis on one or more notes
BOREAL OWL	high-pitched rapid staccato notes
BURROWING OWL	high-pitched "coo, coo"
EASTERN SCREECH OWL	high-pitched tremulous descending whistling screech
ELF OWL	high-pitched rapid staccato notes
FERRUGINOUS PYGMY OWL	high-pitched "hoot" repeated rapidly in long series
FLAMMULATED OWL	single deep-pitched resonant "hoot" repeated at intervals in series
GREAT GRAY OWL	single deep-pitched resonant "hooo" repeated at intervals in series
GREAT HORNED OWL	deep-pitched resonant "hoo, hoo, hooooo, hoo" with emphasis on one or more notes
LONG-EARED OWL	single deep-pitched "hooo" repeated at intervals in series
NORTHERN HAWK OWL	high-pitched, staccato notes
NORTHERN PYGMY OWL	single high-pitched musical note
NORTHERN SAW-WHET OWL	series of ascending metallic notes
SHORT-EARED OWL	drawn-out high-pitched raspy screech
SNOWY OWL	deep-pitched "hoo, hooo" in series or single high-pitched "scree"
SPOTTED OWL	single deep-pitched resonant "hoo" repeated in series of three or four
WESTERN SCREECH OWL	series of "hoo, hoo, hoo" with accelerating tempo, sometimes ending in staccato roll
WHISKERED SCREECH OWL	high-pitched "hoo, hoo, hoo, hoo" in syncopated series

a positive means of identification. Each species has a distinctive style of call. However, these often guttural sounds do not translate well into written descriptions. Most observers note the pattern and frequency of a call as well as its general nature in order to make a positive identification. Audiotapes and CD recordings of North American bird calls provide the best reference (see below).

FOR MORE HELP

Recordings of bird calls are collected and analyzed at the Cornell Laboratory of Ornithology (Ithaca, NY). Audio tapes and compact discs are available from this collection, including almost every species of owl found in North America. More information is available on the World Wide Web at

<http://www.ornith.cornell.edubirdlab.html>

Tapes and CDs can be found at local bookstores or birding outlets, published by:

Peterson Field Guides
Houghton Mifflin Company
120 Beacon Street
Somerville, MA 02143

OWL TERRITORY

"It is during the placid serenity of a beautiful summer night, when the current of the waters moves silently along, reflecting from its smooth surface the silver radiance of the moon, and when all else of animated nature seems sunk in repose, that the Great Horned Owl, one of the Nimrods of the feathered tribes of our forests, may be seen sailing silently and yet rapidly on, intent on the destruction of the objects destined to form his food."
— John James Audubon (*Birds of America*, 1840)

Depending on the species, owls can be extremely territorial or peaceably coexist with others of their kind. The barn owl, for example, can have a hunting territory that greatly overlaps other barn owls, with little aggression shown during normal hunting activity. The immediate vicinity of their nesting sites, however, are vigorously defended. In a few cases, observers have noted multiple pairs of barn owls sharing the same general nesting site, usually a large abandoned building. This kind of colony, however, probably forms because of the suitability of the site for a large number of nests rather than any inclination on the part of the birds to nest together. Owls, unlike penguins or pigeons, rarely live in colonies.

Most owls in North America have overlapping food sources. In other words, more than one type of owl preys upon the same prey animal in its natural range. But there are very few owl species or locations that actively overlap because each species generally favors different hunting and nesting conditions. On any given night, few owls compete against one another for a meal.

The Pacific coast states, from California north to British Columbia, have the highest number of species in the same general area, with eleven species found in the region. In parts of the western states — including Nevada, Utah, and Idaho — up to ten species may be found, a density similar to the isolated mountains and canyons of southern Arizona. For most of the eastern United States, including the midwest and New England, six or seven species is a typical condition, and throughout most of the southern states, four to five species is common.

North American owl species have a variety of responses to threats on their territory. When defending nests with eggs or chicks, most owl species are aggressive and fierce. On the nest site, adult owls will assume a threatening posture, with head lowered, wings spread, and feathers ruffled to increase their apparent size. Threat calls include hisses, clicks made with the bill, and sometimes screeches or screams. Species such as the long-eared owl have been observed attacking intruders, including humans, and may use their talons to swipe at and actually slash the unwanted guest, almost always from the front. When repulsing others of their species, owls may grapple with one another while in the air, talons gripping talons while both birds cartwheel through the sky. Some owls also use a mock injury behavior — folding or drooping one wing — to distract predators away from their nests, although this kind of broken wing behavior is only displayed by species that nest on the ground.

Another kind of response is common with the smallest owl species, including the pygmy owls and the elf owl. Females of these species, startled or threatened while on their nests, may appear to be unconscious, assuming a lifeless posture. This kind of response might be an effective way to avoid danger, because by freezing movement — a trigger for attack in many predators — they eliminate this potential response. Extreme stillness also maximizes the effect of the natural camouflage of the owl's plumage.

Most of the time, owls that remain still when they are mobbed by other birds during perching will also assume a special cryptic posture that maximizes their camouflage, pulling their feathers in close to their bodies, erecting their ear tufts, and closing their eyes. The

OWL HABITATS

DESERT	elf owl, ferruginous pygmy owl
DESERT SCRUB	barn owl, burrowing owl, great horned owl
GRASSLAND	barn owl, burrowing owl, great horned owl, northern saw-whet owl, short-eared owl,
HARDWOOD	barred owl, great gray owl, long-eared owl, northern saw-whet owl
HARDWOOD-CONIFER	whiskered screech owl
LIVE OAKS	long-eared owl
MIXED CONIFER	flammulated owl, great horned owl, northern pygmy owl, northern saw-whet owl, short-eared owl, spotted owl, western screech owl
OPEN WOODS	northern hawk owl
PINON-JUNIPER	flammulated owl, great horned owl, long-eared owl, northern saw-whet owl, western screech owl
PONDEROSA	great horned owl, northern pygmy owl, short-eared owl, spotted owl
RIVER WOODS	long-eared owl
SPRUCE-FIR	flammulated owl, great horned owl, northern pygmy owl, northern saw-whet owl, spotted owl, western screech owl
TUNDRA	snowy owl

large, prominent eyes of owls are, in fact, thought to be one of the major features by which other birds identify them.

Noise is also an effective defense for owls. Screeches, screams, hisses, and bill clicking are used in attempts to discourage intruders or predators. Young burrowing owls have an even more unique vocal weapon — they produce what is called a "rattlesnake rasp," a rattle-like cry that mimics the warning buzz of a rattlesnake's tail. Coming from inside a darkened hole in the ground, the sound once convinced observers that these dangerous snakes lived in the same burrows with the owls. A similar cry has been noted with two tree-nesting owls species, the western screech owl and the northern saw-whet owl.

Owls are often most aggressive toward competing owls that come near or intrude into their own territory. Even when sharing territory, they will occasionally threaten or attack their neighbors, but usually only if the neighbor has come too close to their nest site.

The great horned owl, one of the most widespread species in North America, is noted for its aggressive territorial defense. No other owls of any species are tolerated in the general vicinity of a great horned owl nest, although its overall hunting territory — which may cover more than 1,000 acres — may overlap that of other, noncompeting owl species. But the great horned owl also seems tolerant of other raptors, as long as they aren't owls. Most likely because their normal cycles of activity are opposite, great horned owls are often found nesting close to raptors such as hawks and eagles, in some cases even in the same tree. During the beginning of the breeding season, however, great horned owls are not shy about attacking hawks or eagles in order to steal their nests.

Some owls do not exhibit such defensive behavior. The spotted owl, for example, is noted for its rather passive response to intruders, especially humans. Observers have long noted that many of these owls can be readily approached, even close enough to be grabbed, with few if any signs of alarm or a flight reaction. One explanation is that this species, in its natural range, has so few predators that it has not developed a protective reaction. And the northern spotted owl, a subspecies, may ultimately suffer from this behavior, being less capable of avoiding the increasing threats from logging and other uses of the forest habitats that it favors.

MIGRATION

*"The Scritch Owl alwayes betokeneth some heavie newes
and is most execrable and accursed. In summer he is the
very monster of the night, neither singing nor crying out
cleare, but uttering a certaine heavie groane of doleful
mourning and therefore if it be seene to flie abroad in any
place it prognosticateth some fearful misfortune."*

— Pliny

In North America, only the elf owl, northern saw-whet owl, and flammulated owl have regular migration habits. Their migration routes are not as regular as some other bird species, however, and may even be different on the way north than when headed south. Most likely, their routes are selected due to the availability of food. In different seasons, this may mean different types of rodents or insects, naturally favoring one route over another.

True migration means that birds follow a regular annual flight schedule between two distant regions. But some owls may "migrate" over short distances or follow a more irregular migration pattern, leaving a region in some years but not others. Among barn owls, for example, some birds in the northern part of their natural range are likely to have a migration schedule, while barn owls in the southern region do not seem to migrate at all.

The snowy owl is a frequent winter visitor in northern states of the United States and an occasional visitor much further to the south. The pattern of visitation, however, does not come from regular migration, but from a search for relief from severe weather conditions and lack of food in its normal range far to the north. Some studies of the snowy owls' major food source, lemmings, show that visits to the south are likely to coincide with a natural rhythm in the population size of these northern rodents. Every three to four years, lemming populations peak, then crash, a natural cycle. When the number of lemmings drops dramatically, snowy owls head south. A similar pattern of movement has been observed with great horned owls. In the northern part of their range, great horned owls feed heavily on snowshoe hares, an animal population which peaks on an eight- to ten-year cycle. At the low point for this population, observers in the past have noted an unusually large number of great horned owls in many regions of the United States, far south of the territory favored by snowshoe hares.

Owls that are normally found only in some regions of the country may occasionally appear elsewhere, sometimes far from their normal territory. Sometimes owls that are regular residents of South America, Africa, or Europe have been seen in North America, but these also are not migrations.

Elf owls, which have a regular migration pattern, typically arrive from Mexico in March but occasionally may show up in southwestern states as early as mid-January. They usually leave in September but may occasionally hang around as late as mid-October. Flammulated owls, also regular migrants, arrive from March through April and leave from late September through October. Migration for northern saw-whet owls begins in March; the return south runs from late September to late November.

MOBBING

Smaller birds, at the bottom of the food chain, rarely get the chance to get even with raptors. But owls, as well as eagles and hawks, are frequently targeted by groups of these birds for loud and relentless torment if they are caught in the open or spotted while roosting. In a behavior called *mobbing*, groups of birds attack the owls in continuous waves. These bird groups are informal collections of whatever species happen to be in an area when an owl is spotted. Birds as large as crows and as small as hummingbirds may participate, but songbirds are most common. Mobbing generally consists of repeated dives on the head and body of the owl, accompanied by loud alarm calls. Birds will also sometimes physically pluck at an owl's feathers or eyes and rake it with their claws, but few instances are known of owls actually being harmed. The purpose is not so much to damage the enemy but alert other birds to its presence, and owls generally are not much affected. In one study of eastern screech owls, mobbing was found to have an effect on owls less than half the time. Mostly, owls ignore the attacking birds, compressing their feathers, erecting their ear tufts, and closing their eyes to look less threatening. When they are forced to move, they rarely fly very far, selecting another perch close to their original location. Owls do not counterattack while being mobbed. Even though the attacking birds may represent a source of food, mobbing does not seem to trigger the owls' hunting instincts.

OWL WATCHING

"Now at sundown I hear the hooting of an owl, — hoo hoo hoo, hoorer hoo. It sounds like the hooting of an idiot or a maniac broke loose. ... This is my music each evening."
— Henry David Thoreau (November 18, 1851, *Journal*)

Despite their nighttime habits, owls are a favorite bird among birdwatchers. Unfortunately for the owls, birdwatchers are usually not happy unless they actually see their quarry. Bird watching tradition has developed a more active form for owls than with other birds because of the lack of light during their most active hours. In order to find owls in the dark, the usual practice is to use a prerecorded tape of owl calls to tempt owls into sighting distance, where flashlights or floodlights may be used to illuminate them. In recent years, new infrared or other "night vision" sighting devices have also been adopted by some nighttime birding fans.

The practice of owl calling, although widely used for many years, may be harmful to the lifestyle of many owls. The calls that owls are responding to may be perceived as a threat to their territory and produce aggression and stress. The calls can also chase owls out of their own territory. Particularly with smaller owl species which are preyed upon by larger owls, calls can be particularly threatening. Chasing owls out of their nesting sites pushes them into unfamiliar territory where they may be harmed by resident owls or other predators and may cause some female owls to abandon their nests, eggs, or chicks.

During daytime owl hunts, diligence in locating owl nest sites often brings observers too close to owl nests. This can also be threatening for many owls, causing them to abandon nests and territory permanently.

What is a safe method of enjoying these flying creatures in the wild? Most experts now recommend call identification as the only humane way to "observe" owls in the field. By listening carefully to the natural calls being made by owls — particularly during breeding season — precise identification of species is not only possible, it is the only accurate method for telling some species apart. This may leave some dedicated owl lovers disappointed, but aviaries and zoos throughout the country have many types of owl on display, permitting viewing without disturbing their relatives in the wild.

OWL WATCHING GUIDELINES

- During breeding season, owl watching can be extremely disruptive and threatening to nesting species. Avoid using any type of owl calls during this period.
- The use of taped owl calls is illegal in many areas, including national parks and wildlife preserves.
- Stay as far away as possible from perching owls.
- Handling owl pellets can be extremely unhealthy. Pellets can transmit several diseases, including hantavirus.
- Leave feathers where you find them. Federal wildlife law prohibits possession of the feathers of wild birds.
- For the best results when seeking owls, take advantage of local wildlife resources, including birding clubs, wildlife associations, and natural history museums.

OWL HOUSES

"Little Saw-Whet, the prairie-haunting Short-eared Owl, and the hemlock-loving Long-eared Owl are among the most respectable of American bird citizens."
— George Miksch Sutton
(*Birds in the Wilderness: Adventures of An Ornithologist*, 1936)

At least for the barn owl, civilization has provided some rewards. The same barns, sheds, steeples, and towers that provide them with superior nesting sites come with a regular supply of mice, rats, bats, and other food sources not likely to be appreciated by their human hosts. In rural parts of the Netherlands, farmers traditionally went out of their way to encourage barn owls to take up residence. Special owl doors were added to the gables of barns to encourage barn owls to nest. Known as "uilebords," these doors became part of local barn design, using small round openings high in the gables and sometimes enclosed nesting rooms.

In modern times, declining populations of some owl species have pushed conservationists to develop substitutes for the natural nesting sites that are often in short supply. Platforms, boxes, and artificial cavities have all been used successfully in the wild. Increasingly, the same approach is being taken in rural and suburban locations as more people develop interest in these silent nighttime hunters. Although most urban locations offer little to attract most species of owls, homeowners with large lots and those at the fringes of urban areas may find success with some kinds of owl housing.

Owl species which are most likely to take advantage of a nest box include barn owls and screech owls, but boreal owls, saw-whet owls, barred owls, great horned owls, long-eared owls, and great gray owls have all been known to lay eggs and raise broods in manmade structures.

Larger owl species are less likely to use a nesting box, however large, than a nesting platform. Such open constructions provide the same simple shape and support that owls find in nature, usually already-constructed nest platforms put together by eagles, hawks, crows, or tree squirrels.

The most effective nesting platforms are also the simplest: a few boards to form the base, and on top of this, a shallow container made of chicken wire. Nesting materials such as small branches and leaves are placed in the basket. The platform should be mounted twenty to thirty feet above the ground, either in a tree or on a pole. Especially for great horned owls, an area around the nest must be open to a distance of at least 15 feet and as much as 25 feet to allow for takeoffs and landings.

A thought to ponder. Although owls are universally appealing to wildlife lovers, they can create a dilemma for some wild bird fans. This is because wild birds, including many favorite song birds, are part of the regular diet of many owls. If owls are encouraged to nest in backyards, parks, or near bird feeding or watering stations, it will inevitably lead to the owls following their instincts and selecting meals of convenience, including those birds that are attracted to the free food and water left out for them. Because most owls are completely or primarily nocturnal, however, both support systems may cooexist quietly, if not peaceably.

Barn owls are the most likely owls to be attracted to nesting boxes. Like most owls, they do not make their own nests in the wild, but seek out sheltered overhangs and natural cavities.

OWL HOUSE GUIDELINES

	INTERIOR SIZE	ENTRANCE LOCATION	ENTRANCE DIAMETER	MOUNTING HEIGHT
SAW-WHET OWL	6x6x10"	8-10"	2½"	12-20'
SCREECH OWL	8x8x12"	10"	3"	10-30'
BARN OWL	10x18x18"	4"	6"	12-18'

WHERE TO MOUNT

SAW-WHET OWLS	Trees or poles at the edge of clearings
SCREECH OWLS	Trees or poles at the edge of clearings
BARN OWLS	Trees, poles, sides of buildings

GENERAL GUIDELINES

❏ Locate the entrance hole to the side or in the middle.

❏ Hinge the top or side to allow for periodic cleaning and inspection.

❏ White paint helps reflect heat.

❏ Install with entrance hole sited to the east.

❏ Add nesting material in 1" layer and replace annually (wood shavings or wood chips).

❏ Take care to eliminate or discourage potential predators of owl eggs and young, including tree squirrels and raccoons. Use metal flashing below to reduce climbing access.

❏ Do not disturb nest while in use.

❏ Nest sites are chosen beginning in January. Be patient. It can take months or a few years for nesting box to be discovered.

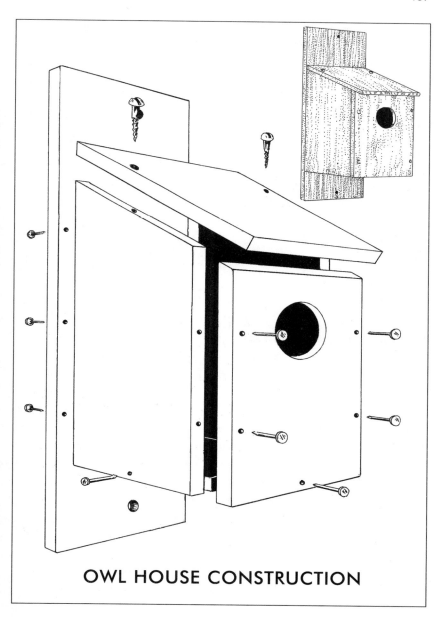

OWL HOUSE CONSTRUCTION

PEOPLE VERSUS OWLS

"When night comes, one may hear the Screech Owl's tremulous, wailing whistle. It is a weird, melancholy call, welcomed only by those who love Nature's voice, whatever be the medium through which she speaks."

— Frank M. Chapman
(Handbook of Birds of Eastern North America, 1934)

Like all birds of prey, owls are a constant focus of attention to birds that might become their prey. During the daytime, roosting owls that are spotted by other birds are often mobbed. It is just this behavior that long ago inspired bird hunters to use owls as decoys. One of the earliest references to this activity comes from Aristotle, who mentioned it in a book written in 350 B.C. To hunt with an owl, a live owl was tied to a stake or branch. As birds arrived to mob the owl, they were trapped with nets, nooses, or sticky material smeared on landing surfaces. In modern times, owls have sometimes been used in a similar way to help reduce the number of crows, birds despised by farmers for their insatiable appetite for grain. As the crows circle a tethered owl, they are shot and killed by concealed hunters.

Barn owls generally have a positive reputation in rural areas. Not large enough to prey upon farm animals such as chickens, these flying predators are credited for focusing their voracious appetites on small rodents, the bane of farmers. A typical barn owl hunts close to the nest, therefore if it resides in a farmer's barn, most of its hunting is concentrated close to the barn. Studies have shown that barn owls usually fly no more than one or two miles from their nest site when in search of food, although they have been known to fly as far as 3½ miles.

Their hunting habits as well as their willingness to live near people make barn owls acceptable to many people. Humans, however, are not what attracts owls, but the rodents that are inevitably con-centrated around the farms people populate. In owl logic, the equa-tion is simple, where there are farmers, there are rodents. In the modern era, more owls have also taken advantage of alterations to the landscape and habitat by suburban and urban dwellers. Street lights and porch lights, for instance, attract insects which then attract insect-eating owls. In some cases, bats that are attracted to the insects for the same reason will become targets of owls. Dense groves of trees that are razed for parks and building developments, while they remove prime nesting territory for some owls, also create improved hunting habitat for others. At the edge of forests where trees meet fields, small rodents, insects, and birds are often most concentrated, providing similar enhanced hunting conditions for the owls.

On an average night, a single adult barn owl will catch and con-sume one or two rodents, but with nesting chicks to feed, the num-ber will be higher. In a single year, a nesting pair can be responsible

ERRONEOUS IDEAS CONCERNING HAWKS AND OWLS

"Much misapprehension still exists among farmers as to the habits of birds of prey. Examination of the contents of the stomachs of such birds, to the number of several thousand, has established the fact that their food consists almost entirely of injurious mammals and insects, and that accordingly these birds are in most cases positively beneficial to the farmer, and should be fostered and protected."

— Yearbook of the United States Department of Agriculture, 1895 for the demise of more than 1,000 rodents. In urban settings, many owls may also prey upon Norway rats, an imported menace that has become a regular part of the city environment.

Owls are found in relative abundance in most parts of North America, but not all owl species are doing well in all areas. In Missouri, for instance, only the great horned owl thrives in a state where four different owl species have had a natural range.

What destructive forces hurt owls? In recent years, it is not the direct killing of owls that is the main threat to their population size, but indirect effects of human activity. Urban sprawl and modern agricultural practices are probably the chief culprits. Urbanization continually chips away at the surviving stands of woods and meadows that provide owls with nesting protection and hunting territory. As trees are removed to make room for shopping malls, housing developments, and fields, the number of nesting sites shrinks. Chemicals used to kill insects and rodents also take a toll. Passing into the digestive system of predators, they can kill outright or accumulate gradually, either reducing the healthiness of the bird or harming the offspring. Even when they are not eaten by owls, the destruction of rodents and other agricultural pests reduces their natural food supply, forcing them into ever smaller territories.

Another deadly force arising from agriculture is mowing and harvesting of feed grasses and the use of field crops for grazing animals. Fields of hay and other crops often reproduce the natural vegetation that ground-nesting owls prefer, and many of these fields lie in geographic zones that have long been favored by these birds. But as cultivation expands, these owls may be plowed under or mowed down along with the crops.

Urban expansion is also a significant force in the reduction of natural habitats, a loss that affects owls and their prey. One study of screech owls, for example, found that only 30 percent of the greenspace within an urban area was suitable for use by the owls. At the same time, urban areas usually become permanent habitats for some kinds of animals that may provide food for owls. Pigeons, starlings, tree squirrels, and rats — all potential food for owls — are some of the wildlife that thrive in urban environments. One of the greatest modern threats to owls comes from vehicles. The openness of streets and highways provides an efficient hunting ground for owls, where the scurrying of small mammals is easily detected. Swooping to snatch prey or stopping to feed on dead animals killed by vehicles, owls themselves fall prey to these deadly machines. Large owls are also a serious hazard at many airports. Attracted by large expanses of relatively undisturbed grasses, rodents thrive, providing a steady draw for owls on the hunt. Collisions with airplanes are common and large owls are enough of a threat to planes to require regular programs of control in order to reduce the problem.

Owls are also killed by electricity. Generally a problem only with the largest species because of their wingspan, encounters with transmission lines and transformers are common, usually killing the bird. In nature, lightning may also have a similar effect, tending to strike the large, lone trees that are favored by many owls because of their nesting potential.

In past eras, some cultures have treated owls as evil, chasing them away or killing them in an attempt to avert danger or death. In arctic regions, native cultures such as the Eskimo have also relied upon at least one owl species — the snowy owl — as a source of food. Snowy owls may have been targeted both because they are one of only a few year-round animals in a harsh environment and because they are the only owl with a high percentage of body fat, perhaps improving the taste and texture of their meat. John James Audubon was one noted early naturalist who commented on this fact. Writing in *Birds of America*, he stated that this bird was "covered with much flesh of a fine and delicate appearance, very much resembling that of a chicken, and not disagreeable eating. ..." Evidence from prehistoric human cultures suggests a fondness for snowy owls may be an old tradition, with some excavated caves in Europe showing that snowy owls represented the greatest percentage of birds consumed by the occupants.

Describing barred owls, Audubon also mentioned finding them for sale in the markets of New Orleans, where they were sold for use as an ingredient in Creole gumbo. Following the Civil War, shortages of food in many areas of the south also pushed owl meat onto the menu, along with many other birds not normally consumed. In Norfolk, Virginia, in 1885, one observer noted seeing at least 400 species of birds for sale — including screech owls — in the city's food markets. Generally, however, owls have not been a regular part of the diet of any culture.

Hunters in previous eras deliberately targeted owls, much as they

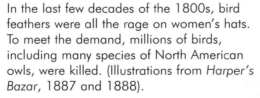

In the last few decades of the 1800s, bird feathers were all the rage on women's hats. To meet the demand, millions of birds, including many species of North American owls, were killed. (Illustrations from *Harper's Bazar*, 1887 and 1888).

did eagles and hawks, because of their predatory attacks on favored hunting prey, including ducks, geese, and many kinds of fur-bearing mammals. Trappers, in particular, fought running battles with owls that took advantage of the easy meals they could grab from traplines. In some cases, trappers deliberately set traps for owls in order to eliminate competition for their commercial operations. This was common until recently on fur farms and poultry operations where animals were raised in open pens. Pole traps were developed for such applications, with steel traps mounted on tall poles, attractive observation platforms for owls, as well as other raptors, looking for a quick meal. These traps are now banned, but some agricultural operations do receive permission to livetrap raptors if they are a nuisance.

In a few parts of the country, some local governments once encouraged the control of owls through the use of special hunting bounties. Legislation in Pennsylvania in 1885, for example, organized a system of payments that gave citizens fifty cents for each owl

An illustration drawn by Bert R. Elliott in 1923 for "The Owl and the Pussycat," a poem by Edward Lear.

they killed. Owls were not singled out, however; the same law offered a similar bounty for other predators, including hawks and weasels. Within a year and a half of the law's enactment, a published report totaled the results: 128,571 animals turned in for bounties, mostly hawks and owls. As late as the early 1960s, when a version of this law was still in effect, more than 1,400 great horned owls were killed for a bounty in a single year.

Owls were not universally despised, however. The earliest national conservationist movements began in the late 1800s as a response to the growing fashion trend that made bird feathers, wings, and entire bodies a coveted part of women's hats and accessories. From about 1880 to 1886, an estimated 5 million birds were caught and killed for their feathers in the United States alone. And not just birds suffered from this fashion affliction — small mammals from weasels to house cats ended up mounted on millinery. At the peak of this trend, some bird lovers got to see more species mounted on hats than they would find in the wild. One observer wrote of spotting 160 species in a few days while strolling the avenues of New York City.

> "Hats will be feather-laden all winter as they have been flower-laden in the summer. ... Owl-heads with wings in natural gray and fancy colors are set just in front of the crown, with wings close along the sides as if brooding."
>
> — *Harper's Bazar,*
> September 6, 1890

The slaughter attracted more than scattered attention from individuals; it ultimately triggered the creation of widespread conservation movements and wildlife protection programs. Whereas most of the birds with the most coveted plumage were songbirds or insect eaters and were widely thought to have no advantage to mankind other than their aesthetic appeal, most owls were recognized as efficient predators of rodents that were a plague to civilization.

To protect owls rather than kill them had positive rewards, especially for farmers. These kinds of observations led to the elimination of organized hunting for most owl species — great horned owls were a notable exception — although bounties were offered well into the middle of the twentieth century for some birds such as crows.

Although throughout history many people seem to have feared and avoided owls, others have been attracted by their uniqueness. Tame owls are a common occurrence in North America, part of a long tradition of wildlife kept as pets. John James Audubon wrote about several tame owls and once carried a screech owl chick in his pocket all the way from Philadelphia to New York City. In 1878, a small town newspaper in Kansas reported of a resident horned owl

Illustration drawn by F. S. Church for
"The Misses Winter's Christmas Party,"
published in *Harper's Bazar*, December 12, 1887.

"which amuses the people there by killing cats as fast as they are handed him."

Owls have been treated much more kindly in literature. Especially in books for children in the past one hundred years, owls have personified wisdom and knowledge.

ENDANGERED OWLS

"As for the aesthetic loss of no longer seeing the Short-eared Owl perform its intricate courtship dance, its brilliant wounded-bird ruse, its soaring, fantastic flights; as for the loss to the poet, the philosopher, the farmer, the teacher, the psychologist, the curious child, and all those who could learn new meanings of love, freedom, devotion, and tolerance from the Bog Trotter's singing wings — this loss is beyond calculation."
— Jonathan Evan Maslow (*The Owl Papers*, 1988)

Barn owls, one of the most common owls in North America, are vulnerable to the expanding threats of civilization. In some parts of the country, populations of barn owls are declining and their future is uncertain. Barn owls are listed by the National Audubon Society as a "species of special concern."

Ferruginous pygmy owls are among the most threatened due to the loss of habitat. Once common in Arizona and parts of Texas, ranching, mining, woodcutting, water diversion, housing development, and other expanding land uses have driven almost all of them out of this part of their range. Favoring dense vegetation along rivers and streams — labeled riparian habitat — it is exactly this type of land that is first to be exploited for human use. According to one estimate, more than 90 percent of all riparian habitat in the southwestern United States has now been destroyed or modified for other uses, removing it from the natural range of this owl, not to mention many other species of animals and plants.

The northern spotted owl has become one of the most notably threatened birds in the United States in recent years. One of the subspecies of spotted owl found in North America, these owls have been severely impacted by widespread logging in regions along the northwest coast. One of the owl species with a traditionally low rate of reproduction success, northern spotted owls are thought to be particularly sensitive to intrusions or changes to their local habitats by human use.

Primarily at home in open ground with few or no trees, short-eared owls have been slowly decreasing in numbers in most of their range in recent decades, a direct result of changes to their natural habitat. Mostly because of agricultural use, land once open to short-eared owls has rapidly been converted to uses that disrupt or displace these birds.

In many regions in its range, the eastern screech owl has been declining in numbers. And the burrowing owl, formerly common and widespread throughout central and western North America, is now declining in numbers in California, Florida, and Canada.

Unfortunately for most of these species, the forces of civilization that are out-competing them are not simple to thwart. In the long run, it is likely that one or more species will disappear throughout its natural range.

RESOURCES

Organizations that deal with bird, animal, and wildlife issues can provide additional information about owls, as well as being useful in local, regional, or national efforts to protect natural habitats and endangered species.

American Birding Association
P.O. Box 6599
Colorado Springs, CO 80934
800-634-7736

National Audubon Society
700 Broadway
New York, NY 10003
212-979-3100

The Nature Conservancy
1815 N. Lynn Street
Arlington, VA 22209
703-841-5300

Owl Magazine
847A Second Avenue, Suite 247
New York, NY 10017
800-860-1100

The Owl's Nest
P.O. Box 990, Depoe Bay, OR 97341
541-765-2473
EMAIL owlsnest@newportnet.com

Owl Research Institute
P.O. Box 8355
Missoula, MT 59807
406-549-7626
EMAIL owl@montana.com

Wild Bird Magazine
3 Burroughs, Irvine, CA 92718
714-855-8822

Hunting for owl pellets? These resources provide safe, reliable quantities of owl pellets for classroom research and other uses. Even with reliable supplies of pellets, remember to use appropriate caution when handling to avoid diseases such as salmonella.

Genesis Inc.
P.O. Box 2242, Mount Vernon, WA 98273
1-800-473-5538

Ward's Natural Science
5100 West Henrietta Road, Rochester, NY 14692-9012
1-800-962-2660

ONLINE RESOURCES

Computer connections to information can prove useful to those interested in wildlife and nature. Online resources include reference material, discussions with like-minded individuals, communications with agencies and organizations involved with wildlife, and access to up-to-date information and schedules. As the online industry is growing and evolving rapidly, listed resources may change and new resources may pop up unexpectedly. To search for additional resources, look for menu listings or search for topics associated with **birds, wildlife, wild animals, nature, ecology,** and **environmental resources.** Also look for topics listed by the common name of an animal, such as **owl.**

Many libraries now provide access to their materials through online connections. Using terminals inside libraries — or dialing in from a remote location — follow the same search strategies to locate books, reference material, and periodicals.

AMERICA ONLINE

Go to <Nature Conservancy> or <Birding>

WORLD WIDE WEB

Owls Nest <http://www.newportnet.com/owlsnest/who.html-ssi>

Owl Research Institute <http://www.montana.com/owl/owl.htm>

Birding on the Web <http://www.birder.com>

Peterson online <http://www.petersononline.com/birds>

Cornell Laboratory of Ornithology
    <http://www.ornith.cornell.edu/birdlab.html>

Smithsonian Migratory Bird Center
    <http://www.si.edu/natzoo/zooview/smbc/smbchome.htm>

BIBLIOGRAPHY

Alcorn, Gordon Dee. *Silent Wings*. 1982, Ye Galleon Press (Fairfield, Washington).

Anker, Jean. *Bird Books and Bird Art*. 1938, Levin and Munksgaard (Copenhagen, Denmark). Republished in 1974 by Arno Press, Inc. (New York, New York).

Armstrong, Edward. *The Folklore of Birds: An Enquiry into the Origin and Distribution of Some Magico-Religious Traditions*, Second Edition. 1970, Dover Publication. Originally published in 1958 by Collins (London, England).

Austing, G. Ronald and Holt, John B. Jr. *The World of the Great Horned Owl*. 1966, J.B. Lippincott Company (Philadelphia, Pennsylvania).

Baird, S.F., Brewer, T.M., and Ridgway, R. *A History of North American Birds, Volume III*. 1874, Little, Brown, and Company.

Benyus, Janine M. *The Field Guide to Wildlife Habitats of the Western United States*. 1989, Fireside Books/Simon & Schuster, Inc.

Bergen, Fanny D., editor. *Animal and Plant Lore: Collected from the Oral Tradition of English Speaking Folk*. 1899, American Folklore Society/Houghton, Mifflin & Co.

Bird, David M., Varland, Daniel E., and Negro, Juan Jose. *Raptors in Human Landscape: Adaptations to Built and Cultivated Environments*. 1996, Academic Press/Harcourt Brace & Company.

Branner, John C. *How and Why Stories*. 1921, Henry Holt & Company.

Bunn, D.S.; Warburton, A.B.; and Wilson, R.D.S. *The Barn Owl*. 1982, Butteo Books (Vermillion, South Dakota).

Burroughs, John. *Wake-Robin*. 1891, Houghton, Mifflin & Company.

Burton, Robert. *Bird Flight: An Illustrated Study of Birds' Aerial Mastery*. 1990, Facts on File.

Choate, Ernest A. *The Dictionary of American Bird Names* (revised edition). 1985, Harvard Common Press. Revised by Raymond A. Paynter, Jr.

Craighead, John J. and Craighead, Frank C., Jr. *Hawks, Owls, and Wildlife*. 1956, Wildlife Management Institute and Stackpole Company. Republished in 1969 by Dover Publications Inc.

Davis, John W.; Anderson, Roy C.; Karstad, Lars; Trainer, Daniel O., eds. *Infectious and Parasitic Diseases of Wild Birds*. 1971, Iowa State University Press (Ames, Iowa).

Davison, Verne E. *Attracting Birds: From the Prairies to the Atlantic*. 1967, Thomas Y. Crowell Company.

Dolan, Edward F. *Animal Folklore from Black Cats to White Horses*. 1992, Ivy Books (New York, New York).

Doughty, Robin W. *Feather Fashions and Bird Preservation: A Study in Nature Protection*. 1975, University of California Press (Berkeley, California).

Eckert, Allan W. *The Owls of North America*. 1974, Doubleday & Company.

Ehrlich, Paul R.; Dobkin, David S.; and Wheye, Darryl. *Birds in Jeopardy: The Imperiled and Extinct Birds of the United States and Canada*. 1992, Stanford University Press.

Ehrlich, Paul R.; Dobkin, David S.; and Wheye, Darryl. *The Birder's Handbook: A Field Guide to the Natural History of North American Birds*. 1988, Fireside Books/Simon & Schuster.

Everett, Michael. *A Natural History of Owls*. 1977, Hamlyn Publishing Group Ltd.

Feduccia, Alan. *The Origin and Evolution of Birds*. 1996, Yale University Press (New Haven, Connecticut).

Forbush, Edward Howe. *Natural History of the Birds of Eastern and Central North America*. 1939, Houghton Mifflin Company.

Forsman, Eric D.; DeStefano, Stephen; Raphael, Martin G.; and Gutierrez, R.J., editors. *Demography of the Northern Spotted Owl* (Studies in Avian Biology #17). 1996, Cooper Ornithological Society (c/o Western Foundation of Vertebrate Zoology, Amarillo, California).

Gehlbach, Frederick R. *The Eastern Screech Owl: Life History, Ecology, and Behavior in the Suburbs and Countryside*. 1994, Texas A&M Press (College Station, Texas).

Goodnow, David. *How Birds Fly*. 1992, Periwinkle Books (Columbia, Maryland).

Gotch, A.F. *Birds: Their Latin Names Explained*. 1981, Blanford Press (United Kingdom).

Grossman, Mary Louise and Hamlet, John. *Birds of Prey of the World*. 1964, Clarkson N. Potter, Inc.

Gruson, Edward S. *Words for Birds: A Lexicon of North American Birds with Biographical Notes*. 1972, Quadrangle Books (New York, New York).

Gubernatis, Angelo de. *Zoological Mythology*. 1872, Trübner and Company (London). Republished in 1968 by Singing Tree Press (Detroit, Michigan).

Harrison, Colin. *A Field Guide to the Nests, Eggs, and Nestlings of North American Birds*. 1978, Collins (New York, New York).

Harrison, Hal H. *A Field Guide to Western Birds' Nests*. 1979, Houghton Mifflin Company.

Heintzelman, Donald S. *Guide to Owl Watching in North America*. 1984, Winchester Press/New Century Publishers, Inc. (Piscataway, New Jersey). Republished in 1992 by Dover Publications (Mineola, New York).

Heintzelman, Donald S. *Hawks and Owls of North America*. 1979, Universe Books (New York, New York).

Holmgren, Virginia C. *Owls in Folklore and Natural History*. 1988, Capra Press (Santa Barbara, California).

Howard, Richard and Moore, Alick. *Complete Checklist of the Birds of the World*, 2nd edition. 1991, Academic Press.

Howell, N.G. and Webb, Sophie. *A Guide to the Birds of Mexico and Northern Central America*. 1995, Oxford University Press.

Ingersoll, Ernest. *Birds in Legend, Fable and Folklore*. 1923, Longmans, Green and Company (New York, New York). Republished in 1968 by Singing Tree Press (Detroit, Michigan).

Jobes, Gertrude. *Dictionary of Mythology, Folklore, and Symbols*. 1961, Scarecrow Press.

Jobling, James A. *A Dictionary of Scientific Bird Names*. 1991, Oxford University Press.

Johnsgard, Paul A. *North American Owls: Biology and Natural History*. Smithsonian Institute Press.

Jones, John Oliver. *Where the Birds Are: A Guide to All 50 States and Canada*. 1988, William Morrow and Company Inc.

Leahy, Christopher. *The Birdwatcher's Companion: An Encyclopedic Handbook of North American Birdlife*. 1982, Hill and Wang.

Mahnken, Jan. *The Backyard Bird-Lover's Guide*. 1996, Storey Communications, Inc. (Pownal, Vermont).

Martin, Laura C. *The Folklore of Birds*. 1993, Globe Pequot Press (Old Saybrook, Connecticut).

Maslow, Johnathan Evan. *The Owl Papers*. 1983, Dutton. Republished 1988, Vintage Books/Random House.

Matthews, F. Schuyler. *Fieldbook of Wild Birds and Their Music*. 1904, G.P. Putnam.

Medlin, Faith. *Centuries of Owls in Art and the Written Word*. 1967, Silvermine Publishers Inc. (Norwalk, Connecticut).

Mercatante, Anthony S. *Zoo of the Gods: Animals in Myth, Legend and Fable*. 1974, Harper & Row.

National Geographic Society. *Field Guide to the Birds of North America, Second Edition*. 1987, National Geographic Society.

Nero, Robert W. *The Great Gray Owl: Phantom of the Northern Forest*. 1980, Smithsonian Institution Press.

Newton, Alfred. *A Dictionary of Birds*. 1899, Adam and Charles Black (London).

Nye, William Sturtevant. *Bad Medicine and Good: Tales of the Kiowa*. 1962, University of Oklahoma Press (Norman, Oklahoma).

Ossa, Helen. *They Saved Our Birds: The Battle Won the War to Win*. 1973, Hippocrene Books (New York, New York).

Parson, Elsie Clews. *Pueblo Indian Religion*. 1939, University of Chicago Press. Republished 1966 by Bison Books/University of Nebraska Press (Lincoln, Nebraska).

Peterson, Roger Tory. *A Field Guide to Western Birds*, Second Edition. 1961, Houghton Mifflin Company.

Radford, Edwin and Radford, M.A. *Encyclopedia of Superstitions*. 1949, Philosophical Library (New York, New York).

Reed, Chester A. *North American Birds Eggs*. 1904, Doubleday, Page & Company.

Reichel-Dolmatoff, Gerardo. *Amazonian Cosmos: The Sexual and Religious Symbolism of the Tukano Indians*. 1971, University of Chicago Press. Translated from the original edition, in Spanish, published in 1968 by Universidad de los Andes and Editorial Revista Colombiana Ltd. (Bogota, Columbia).

Robin, P. Ansell. *Animal Lore in English Literature*. 1932, John Murray (London, U.K.).

Root, Terry. *Atlas of Wintering North American Birds: An Analysis of Christmas Bird Count Data*. 1988, University of Chicago Press.

Rowland, Beryl. *Birds with Human Souls*. 1978, The University of Tennessee Press (Knoxville, Tennessee).

Rüppell, Georg. *Bird Flight*. 1977, Van Nostrand Reinhold Company. Originally published in 1975 as *Vogelflug* by Kinder Verlag GmbH (Munich, Germany).

Sayre, James Kedzie. *North American Bird Folknames and Names*. 1996, Bottlebrush Press (Foster City, California).

Sparks, John and Soper, Tony. *Owls: Their Natural and Unnatural History*. 1989, Facts On File.

Stuart, Jozefa. *The Magic of Owls*. 1977, Walker and Company.

Taylor, Iain. *Barn Owls: Predator–Prey Relationships and Conservation*. 1994, Cambridge University Press.

Tyler, Hamilton A. and Phillips, Don. *Owls by Day and Night*. 1978, Naturegraph Publishers, Inc. (Happy Camp, California).

Van Tyne, Josselyn and Berger, Andrew J. *Fundamentals of Ornithology* (second edition). 1976, John Wiley & Sons.

Voous, Karel H. *Owls of the Northern Hemisphere*. 1988, MIT Press (Cambridge, Massachusetts).

Walker, Deward E., Jr. *Blood of the Monster: The Nez Perce Coyote Cycle*. 1994, High Plains Publishing Company (Worland, Wyoming).

Walker, James R. *Lakota Belief and Ritual*. 1991, University of Nebraska Press (Lincoln, Nebraska).

Weeks, Rupert. *Pachee Goyo: History and Legends from the Shoshone*. 1981, Jelm Mountain Press (Laramie, Wyoming).

Wilson, Alexander. *American Ornithology*. 1840, Otis, Broaders, & Co. (Boston, Massachusetts).

INDEX